SKINNY
WOMEN
ARE EVIL

SKINNY WOMEN ARE EVIL

NOTES OF A BIG GIRL IN A SMALL-MINDED WORLD

MO'NIQUE
AND SHERRI A. McGEE

ATRIA BOOKS
New York London Toronto Sydney

ATRIA BOOKS
1230 Avenue of the Americas
New York, NY 10020

ISBN: 0-7434-6471-0
    0-7432-4456-7 (Pbk)

First Atria Books trade paperback edition April 2004

10 9 8 7 6 5 4 3 2 1

ATRIA BOOKS is a trademark of Simon & Schuster, Inc.

Manufactured in the United States of America

For information regarding special discounts for bulk purchases,
please contact Simon & Schuster Special Sales at 1-800-456-6798 or
business@simonandschuster.com

This book is dedicated to Shalon. During the rough times, you wiped away my tears and made me smile. And when the road got rocky, you always found a way to smooth it out for mommy. You are my heart and my soul, and everything I do is for you. Thank you for the many sacrifices you've made. You are mom's little hero.

Stevie, you are one of the most intelligent, incredible men in my life. I am honored to call you my brother. Back in the day when they told us it couldn't be done, you went out and made it happen. Thanks for making it ten times greater.

MO'NIQUE'S ACKNOWLEDGMENTS

First and foremost, I thank God. Mommy and Daddy, you are my rock. Millicent, thanks for the sisterhood and for all of your assistance. Gerald, thanks for teaching me not to take no shit from nobody. Lisa, Michelle, and Yolanda, thanks for over twenty-five years of friendship, and for helping me whip ass and, in the process, get a few ass-whippings, too. Special thanks to my sisterfriend Charisse "Pooh" Smith, who from the time we were seven years old allowed me to be me and listened as I shared my dreams of being a star. I know you're in heaven watching over me and still listening. My aunts Bessie and Tina, thanks for teaching me how to cuss and how to do those combination cusswords. Ms. Ronda Bell, my sisterfriend, thanks for being there and for dressing me in your wonderful fashions all these years. Catherine and Gary, thanks for helping to bring another one of my dreams, of owning a clothing line, to reality. My sister-in-law, Mrs. Kelly Imes, thank you so much for standing in our corner even when your legs got too weak to stand. Special thanks to Kenny "Big Poppa" Young. To my sisters in the Queens of Comedy— Sommore, Adele, and Miss Laura—we made history, y'all. To the road managers on the tour, Tony, Kevin, and Bill, you're the best. To the radio stations around the country who've always shown me nothing but love—thank you. Steve Harvey, you and I have a special friendship. But I'm still going to kick your ass, 'cause I ain't scared of you. Sonny Andre, thanks for pushing for me to get my first radio job. You are my heart. My agent and sisterfriend, Suzy Unger Pulse, when everybody said no, you said yes. A BIG thank-you to my wonderful team at William Morris Agency: Jennifer Craig, Jenean Glover, Stacy Mark, and Mark Itkin. Mark, thank you for your smile. Like you always say, "When the highs are high, they're really high." Oh, and you still owe me a night of dancing. Mrs. Sara Finney-Johnson, not only are you the greatest executive producer I know, but you are an incredible human being. I thank God for you. To the writing team of *The Parkers*, thanks for bringing Nikki Parker to life. Dorien Wilson, thanks for the brotherhood and for helping me learn to share. Yvette Wilson, thanks for always making me look up (it ain't real). And to the rest of my *Parkers* family, I love y'all. To my grandmother Mimmie, thanks for always making me feel important. Grendma, you were, and always will be, the strength of this family. God rest your soul. To my spiritual mother Ms. Eddie (my Nan), thanks for your prayers and always letting me know that God is the answer. I love you. Sheila and Toni, thanks for making me look beautiful all the time. For those who have tried to block my path, thank you, you made me fight harder and become stronger. Tony Singletary, my super director and friend, thank you for your patience, love, and support, and for always giving me your ear. To my acting coach and friend, Mrs. Chip Hurd, thank you for giving me my acting wings. I couldn't have learned from a better teacher. Mr. Manie Barron, you know you are a bad boy for getting us this deal. This is the first of many. To everyone at Atria Books, thanks for believing in this project. Demond Jarrett, thanks for your enthusiasm from day one, and for sharing our proposal with another FLUFFY girl for laughs. More crab on the way. And last, but certainly not least, Ms. Sherri McGee, sister, I really don't think words can express how I feel, but let me try. You are my sisterfriend, my hands, and my voice; you have helped Stevie and I accomplish another chapter in our dreams. Thank you for helping to create and put this book together, and now, let's go straight to the best-seller list.

SHERRI A. McGEE'S ACKNOWLEDGMENTS

First and foremost, I thank God, from whom all blessings flow.

To my parents, Mary and John W. McGee, I'm blessed to have your unconditional love and support. Daddy, you instilled, a la Billie Holiday, "God bless the child who has got her own"—thanks for teaching me well. Mommy, you've always been my biggest fan. What you may not have known is that I am yours, too.

To my new sister, Mo'Nique, thank you for being a part of my dream. We were destined to be friends. I love you, and it was a pleasure to bring your thoughts and feelings to the pages of this book. Let's do it again soon. Steven Imes, you've got to be the hardest-working and best-dressed (besides Rushion McDonald) manager in Hollywood. I am eternally grateful for your belief in my talents.

Special thanks to everyone at Atria Books: Demond Jarrett, our cool, laid-back editor, thanks for "getting it" right away. You made this project fly, and when you were done, Staci Shands, thanks for hooking up the greatest book tour ever. Manie "Big Daddy" Barron, William Morris agent extraordinaire, a million thanks still wouldn't do it, but let me try. Thank you for responding to the query for this book so quickly, and for guiding us through the process. Thank you for the early-morning phone calls with tons of questions, the weekend chats with tons of questions, and for helping us shape this book into a fun read.

God places angels in our lives, and I'm so blessed He placed you in mine, Sara Finney-Johnson. You're more than a boss. You're also my mentor and friend. To my *Parkers* family: Bill, Andrea, Gary, Stacey E. M., Michelle, Stacey Mc., Dornita, Sarah, Patrice, Teri, Kellie, Nancy, Joan, Rocky, Vannika, Rob, LaMar, Marvin, JB, Stephen, Brian, Tony, Larry, Angela, and Melody, not many folks can laugh as much as we do at work. Thanks for making it such a special place. A BIG thanks goes to you, too, Regis Saffold. There's no way we could do it without your assistance. It's always first-rate.

I would like to express appreciation, love, and thanks to my extended family: Grandmother Doris Smith, thanks for always making me feel special. Grandmother Caroline, though I never knew you, you're always in my heart. Granddaddy Ellis Smith, I know you're in heaven smiling down on us. Grandfather John W. McGee, I wish you were here. Uncles Ellis, Lee, Quenion, and George, you're more like big brothers than uncles, and I love you. Uncle Charles, I wish you hadn't left us so soon. Aunts Ruth, Donna, Ollie O, and Miss Bill (the gumbo queens), thanks for your love and support. Cousins Hardy, Doris, Nicole, Lil Tony, Big Tony, Derrick, Kerry, LaDeamya, Zack and Delanda, Terry, Destiny, Du'Mauriea, Lasondra, Alana, Lauren, and Cynthia, thanks for the memories.

A BIG shout-out goes to my sisters circle: Wendy Turner-Codwell, Stacey Evans Morgan, Cheryl Chisholm, Tamara "Buffy" Landry, Chrystal Evans, Camille Tucker, Kim Greene, Tiffany Avery-Smith, Maria Guerrero-Freeman, Dominique Jennings, Kimberly Adams, Debra Colquit, Diann Valentine, Kimberly Ellis, Dawn Baskerville, and Patti Webster.

And last but certainly not least, Anthony, you came along at the perfect moment, and I'm truly thankful for your friendship, love, and support.

CONTENTS

FOREWORD BY WHOOPI GOLDBERG

Look, you need to put aside whatever you think you know about big girls, who they are, what they think, what they're about. You know nothing.

Mo'Nique has written a funny and moving book about how we treat one another, and why no one has to take anyone else's crap anymore. Mo'Nique tells you much more than you ever thought, and has broken down for everyone the joy of loving yourself. And I don't mean faint praise given to oneself to feel better, I'm talking about "Look here, I am, I said."

Mo'Nique has her eyes open and she's gonna open your eyes, too. Don't go thinking that you have nothing in common with her; she is every woman, and every woman waiting to be. The only real difference between you and her is this: She had no real guide; she worked it out. You, you're ahead of the game—you have her.

What you're holding in your hands tells you how she did it. It's a map, a guide to getting on the good foot; grabbing life by the pork chops, taking the biggest attitude you can and saying, "Okay, now I'm me, who the hell are you anyway?"

So get comfortable, honey, 'cause after readin' *Skinny Women Are Evil*, you're not gonna be the same.

ONE

Can't We All Just Get Along?

THE TROUBLE WITH SKINNY WOMEN

I REALLY WISH I DIDN'T have to write this book, but it appears I have no choice. Especially when BIG girls are still subjected to ridicule simply because we've been blessed with a few extra pounds. It's no secret that I am a BIG girl. Always have been. Always will be. Hell, Ray Charles and Stevie Wonder could see that. Which means that the only way I'll ever wear a size six, or even a sixteen, is if you add them together. That's right. I wear a size twenty-two. And I'm proud, because I wear it extremely well. I've never had a problem with my doubles—double chin and double belly. I've also never had a battle with the bulge. Oh, we may have had a few choice words every now and then, but it was always after some stupid he say/she say bullshit. What I've enjoyed is a lifelong love affair with every roll, every lump, and every curve. And because I love me, I've never felt the need to apologize for being my BIG, BEAUTIFUL self.

But it's hard to be a glamour puss when there are forces in the universe that don't believe BIG girls have a right to showcase our assets. They think we should cover up and wear muumuus. Well, I've got two words to say about that—hell no! Why should I hide all this loveliness under big-ass tent dresses? It must be showcased as the masterpiece—of lovely legs, perky breasts, and the dazzling derriere—that it is.

You probably think I'm just paranoid. And saying to yourself, Mo'Nique, girl, stop trippin'. But I've seen the enemy, even witnessed their schemes firsthand, and I'm convinced that the troops on this mission have one goal in mind— TOTAL DOMINATION. That's why fighting them will be tough. They're a powerful, nimble, and wicked bunch, and damn it, they aren't about to go down without a fierce fight. The enemy is on a seek-and-destroy assignment for total destruction—and BIG girls are the targets. You may be wondering, who could be so petty, so treacherous, so damn evil?

SKINNY BITCHES.

Yes, you read right.

And skinny bitches know who they are. If your dress size is in the single digits, chances are I'm talking to you. You're evil and need to be destroyed. I know because for years, I thought they were my friends, but as time rolled on, it soon became clear that these evil bitches didn't give a damn about my feelings. It was always all about them. Well, not if we destroy them, or perhaps trick them with a one-day all-you-can-eat salad special, round them up, and ship their tiny asses off to a sandy island with nothing green on it, just wall-to-wall fried chicken and fast food. That shit would drive them as crazy as they make me and other BIG girls. Don't you hate it when they say stupid shit like, "You need to do something about that gut," and "Isn't that your fourth slice of sweet potato pie?"

No, bitch, it's my fifth, and I may go for a sixth. It's idiotic stuff like that and passing the purses and jackets to me whenever we hit the club, like I'm some damn coat-check girl, that makes me hate them. Hello? Men like BIG girls, too. That's probably why we've got brothers standing in line—plenty of them—and their skinny asses can't get a return phone call. At the mall, they'd walk fast just to see if I could keep up. So you know what I did? Sat my tired ass down and slowed up the entire shopping day. And they loved to taunt me with skimpy outfits I couldn't possibly squeeze one thigh into. So I'd buy three and sew them together. Bottom line. Skinny women are the most intolerant, competitive, judgmental, shallow, sharp-tongued creatures to walk the face of the earth. They play too many damn games and put the PORTLY down in the process. Just because we like to get our eat on doesn't mean there shouldn't be room in the spotlight for us to shine, too. I guess nibbling lettuce cups and tofu steaks makes folks do some hateful shit.

That's why you won't catch a skinny bitch apologizing for being too damn thin. Hell, no. They eat sugarless cake to celebrate it. Well, if those toothpicks can celebrate their minimal assets, then I'm going to flaunt this mega-masterpiece, too, all 220 pounds of it. Shit, I'm so FLUFFY and FABULOUS that if I were to walk into a room with Iman, Naomi, Tyra, and even that original skinny bitch, Barbie, I'd strut my stuff with the grace, finesse, and attitude of the world's finest high-fashion supermodel. That's right! Those trees haven't got shit on me, except maybe an eating disorder. Yes, I'm HEAVY, but I'm also HEALTHY and HAPPY.

Happy to be a THICK girl in an image-conscious industry who's ready to shake some shit up and squash haters that attempt to box me in. Shoot, there ain't a box BIG enough to

The Parkers really is like my family.
This is a publicity photo of us: (l-r) Dorien Wilson, Yvette Wilson,
Ken Lawson, Countess Vaughn, Jenna Von Oy.

hold this gift. Skinny women will not get over at our expense. No more talk shows hosted by skinny bitches who proclaim, "You're too fat to wear that." We've got to put a BIG-ass plan in place to eliminate them. And while it may sound harsh, maybe even cruel, what are BIG girls to do? Get even, of course. Armed with a FULL stomach, and a fuck-them-if-they-ain't-feeling-me attitude, I set out to destroy those who cause FAT folks turmoil, and help other BIG girls tired of hearing, "Are you pregnant?" No, bitch. I'm FAT. It's finally time for us to get some respect. Take our place in the spot-light. Represent. Fight the evil bitches determined to keep us down. But too often, all we hear about is how it's in to be stick-thin. What the hell is so attractive about ribs sticking through skin? Not a damn thing. Now, ribs sticking off the side of a plate, slathered in barbecue sauce, that's a beautiful sight. So is a cute, CURVY girl who knows how to work her shit. Because no one but a dog wants a bone, and even Fido wants one with some damn meat on it. But turn on the televi-sion and all you see is bones, like that Ally McBeal, who I think could have used a McMeal from McDonald's. That's probably why her feeble ass used to fall out every week. She was faint from a lack of food. Thank God she's gone.

That's one down and many more to go. It's time for the skinny sense of superiority to end—for the stronghold to be broken and the grip loosened. Besides, how do those walking knitting needles think they're gonna keep us down? Do they plan to crochet nets to trap us in? Good luck. Because as a BIG girl with an even BIGGER mouth, I'm ready to lead the WIDE way, make a BOLD statement, especially in Hollywood where the skinny starve their way to stardom while that other FAT lady is waiting to sing. Well, let me clear my throat, because this FAT lady is warming up to throw down a PHAT rap called "Skinny Bitch, Give Me the Damn Mic." And I've got a lot to say about how the PLUMP, FULL-FIGURED, OVERWEIGHT—ah, hell, let's just call it like it is, FAT—are treated. Yes, BIG girls, I said FAT. But, don't get nervous, because FAT is only a bad word if you allow it to be. What it really stands for is FABULOUS AND THICK. So, the next time someone calls you FAT, just say thank you and keep those pounds moving. Shoot, girl, don't worry about them words. Because we're taking them back and slapping our BIG-ass seal of approval on them. Since when did a woman who possesses the total package—strength, beauty, and a great body—become PHAT (Pretty, Hot, And Tempting)? Since a skinny bitch got ahold of the shit. You can dress it up, respell it, and make it stand for whatever you want, but the shit is still pronounced F-A-T. And since we're respelling things, then I say PHAT stands for Pretty, Hot And Thick. So chew on that. They can't hurt us with our own shit.

As you read this book, you'll see a few choice adjectives emphasized in BIG letters. It's not a mistake. Just like us, those words are LARGE and LOVELY for a reason. So get comfortable with the descriptions. Embrace them, my BIG sisters. Things must change, not only in tiny-ass Tinseltown but in every town across America, and now that I'm here, its about to get THICK.

A few years ago, folks doubted that a HEAVY honey could make it in Hollywood. They said I'd never be the star of a show. Well, I've got three words to say about that nonsense— kiss my . . . well, you know. My motto is either love this BIG ass, or see you later, 'bye. Life is too damn short and food is too damn good to waste time trying to convince folks that I'm worthy of respect simply because the day the good Lord chose to pass out extra helpings of hips and ass, I thought it was a buffet and got in line twice. Okay, maybe it was more like three or four times, but so what. Hell, it was free—and it looked good.

And isn't that what life is about, anyway, looking good, living well, and eating what you want? You damn right it is. Well, baby, Mo'Nique's got meals to eat, money to meet, sex to get, and skinny bitches to check. Like one skinny agent who told me the best I could hope for in Hollywood were roles as the FAT neighbor, the FAT cousin, or the FAT mother, but never the star. Did she think she was saying something new? Did she really believe this was my first FAT fight? Hell, no. And it damn sure wasn't going to be the last. What she failed to realize is that this star was born long before she stepped foot in Hollywood. I've been waiting all my life for this moment, and I'm not about to let a skinny bitch ruin it. But trying to explain to this bulimic agent that BIGNESS isn't something that just happened to me would take far too long, and so would waiting for her to pull her finger out of her throat. So I told her to stop gagging, move the fuck out of my way, and watch a BIG girl shine. I promise you, my F.A.T. sisters, that together we will conquer small-minds that attempt to limit our abilities. We will be the love interest and the music video hotties. We will be the BIG-assed STARS God meant for us to be. Which means if that Popeye's five-piece chicken dinner (and I'm not talking just wings, either) is calling my name, I'll be able to send some skinny assistant to get my shit. Might even have her fetch me a LARGE strawberry soda, and a slice—or two—of sweet potato pie, too. And I better not hear any shit about it.

Folks don't know it, but I will call in some MEATY mamas and stage a BIG boycott if they don't start adding a few more nonsalad items to menus in this crazy town. Fuck losing five

dress sizes to fit into Hollywood. Hollywood is going to have
to expand to accommodate the millions of BIG, beautiful, talented women out there. All this loveliness is coming—and I'm
bringing Star Jones, Camryn Manheim, Iyanla Vanzant,
Loretta Devine, Emme, Queen Latifah, and my girl Oprah—
whether skinny folks like it or not. I'm on a CHUBBY charge
and calling on all DOUBLE-DIGIT sisters who are
CHUNKY yet FUNKY, FLUFFY and FABULOUS, and
refuse to accept size as a limitation to join the struggle. It matters not the creed or color. All that matters is that you're prepared to fight the FAT fight. It's time we begin to give to
skinny women the same shit they give to us—a headache.
Don't change your behind, BIG girls, just your mind. And
please, eat up, because strength is essential for this mission. If
it feels like a Red Lobster evening, order the FATTEST lobster you can get your hands on. But step your FLUFFY ass
into that restaurant and do it in the nicest two-piece pantsuit
in your closet. Show evil bitches that PLUS-SIZE sisters are
about so much more than the sum of our parts.

I began the first part of my life as a nine-pound baby,
December 11, 1967, in Baltimore, Maryland, the fourth child
born to Steven and Alice Imes. From the time my parents
brought me home from the hospital, friends thought they had
gotten the wrong baby. Surely this CHUNKY child didn't
belong in a slender family of five. Folks assumed what I had
was a temporary bout of baby FAT. Well, that was thirty-five
years ago, and the baby FAT grew up right along with everything else. There ain't nothing baby about it no more, this is
me. As a child, I didn't see too many FAT role models. That is,
until Oprah Winfrey came to town. When Miss O became an
anchor of the local news, I remember thinking, Wow, who's
this sister? She was FAT, she was black, and damn it, even her

I was fortunate to be a part of *The Vagina Monologues*
with three talented sisters: Ella Joyce, Vanessa Bell-Calloway,
and Wendy Raquel Robinson.

Afro was HUGE. Girlfriend may have been BIG but she's brilliant. For the first time, I reasoned that if this BIG girl could make it on television, then I could, too. I liked the fact that Oprah could deliver the news with flair and professionalism, then sit down for a fabulous T-bone steak with all the fixings. I was proud, because here was a sister who'd broken through, and she did it in a BIG-girl way—wearing BIG hair, BIG clothes, and BIG feet too. Finally folks could see that smart people didn't all wear a size six. Some of us wore sixteens. At that point in life, I didn't know what path I'd take to get to the top, but I always knew that I'd be a star, and I pursued entrepreneurial avenues that allowed me to shine. In Oprah, I saw myself.

That is, until the fateful Calvin Klein incident, when girlfriend dieted herself down to nothing and tricked BIG girls. We didn't know whether to eat or not eat. Exercise or not exercise. BIG girls reasoned that if Oprah slimmed down, then, damn it, we had to, too. Especially when she sashayed her happy ass onstage in a pair of Calvin Klein jeans, pulling a wagon of FAT that symbolized all the weight she'd lost. Oprah cheered. The audience cheered. But girlfriend's weight-loss antics didn't move me. It made me mad. What was wrong with representing for SIZABLE sisters? I bet that skinny girlfriend of hers, Gayle, was somewhere in the background cheering her on, too. If some shit is amiss, there's usually a skinny bitch behind it. All at once, Oprah went from being a member of the BIG and BEAUTIFUL to the skinny and skeletal. Since Miss O had abandoned us, someone else would have to champion the BIG cause. So I decided to take up the FAT fight, blow the whistle, and divulge the wicked tricks of the skinny.

I first recognized skinny schemes on the playground in elementary school. I may have been CHUBBY, but my parents told me from an early age that I could do whatever I set my mind to. In fact, my father, bless his heart, told me I was the prettiest little girl in the world. I believed him then—and still do. But those skinny little girls were cruel. Every day it was some new trick. First they accused me of kicking the ball too hard, then complained there wasn't enough room to play in the sandbox with me in it, and snickered if I even ventured toward the monkey bars. They called me Jelly-Belly, Shamu, and even CHUNKY Butt, and piled up on one side of the see-saw because they swore it was impossible to get down with me on the other side. (Some of your eyes may be filling up with tears from the memories, but don't cry, BIG girls. Just hold on, because there's a new sheriff in town.) I may have been BIG, but those evil monsters hurt my little feelings. And since they wouldn't let me in the clique, I had no choice but to settle the score. If it was war those tiny tots wanted, then damn it, it was war they were gonna get. With the seesaw as a launching pad, I got those skinny bitches in the air, then jumped off and watched as they tumbled to the ground like blocks. Just because we had to shop for my school clothes in the HUSKY girls department didn't give them the right to tease me, or snicker at the submarine sandwich, Cheetos, Reese's Peanut Butter Cups, and Twinkies my mother packed in my lunch every day. Shit, it took a lot to keep this body powered.

By the time I got to Milford Mill Academy High School, those skinny little girls had grown into skinny cheerleaders. And every year was the same old story. I'd try out for the squad, only to be told, "Mo'Nique, you were great, but we decided to go with someone else." Damn it, do you know how hard it is to get 200 pounds up in the air? I should have made the squad for that trick alone. I'd be out of breath, and they just snickered. Well, their snickering stopped when, dressed sharp as shit every day, I became the life of the party, the girl-friend of the flyest boy on campus, and by senior year voted Most Popular and Best Dressed. That's right—not the sinister six, or the evil eight, but the enchanting eighteen. YOU CAN'T KEEP BIG GIRLS DOWN!

That's why I need a few million of you to be down with the FAT fight. BIG girls get ready, because there are many components to this mission. First, you've got to get off the sofa, stretch. Next, throw away (my bad—rather, put down) that pint of Ben & Jerry's Chunky Monkey ice cream. Then, I want you to head to the closet and get all dolled up. Strap on a pair of the cutest shoes in your closet, then step out of the house. So what if your feet spill over the sides just a bit, and you stumble at first? Just keep on stepping. And you better step proudly, too. Hold your head up high. Refuse to allow folks to snicker when a HEFTY honey shows up in a miniskirt that has creeped up in the back (due to extra JUNK IN THE TRUNK, also known as bootie-age. No, that shit isn't a word, but those of you who've got it know what it means). Shut them down if they so much as make a moo sound as we bypass the salad bar and head straight to the carving station at the buffet, or laugh hysterically at a your-mama's-so-fat joke. Which, by the way, has caused many a skinny-bitch beat-down. If you must shop with the enemy, fuck that shop-till-you-drop bullshit. Shop till you're hungry, then head straight to the food court for a Krispy Kreme doughnut—you've got to keep your blood sugar up to run through a damn mall all day. Begin to check the insensitive at every level, like I had to when a skinny bitch offered everyone peach cobbler at the party but me. I waited patiently, and when she was done, asked where mine was. Her skinny ass chirped, "Oh, Mo, I thought you were on a diet." Why, because I'm FAT? I shot back, "Well, shit, you look like a starving child from a third-world country, but you don't see me trying to shove food down your throat, do you?" Once skeletons get a taste of their own medicine, trust me, shit will change. Recognize evilness and correct it accordingly. Don't let a few names like tubby, blimp, huge, hefty, husky, two-tons-of-fun, bulky, ample, sizable, whale, and my all-time favorite, chunky butt, shut you down. Sure, name-calling is wrong, but in the game of total domination, the skinny will pull out all the stops. And name-calling is usually their first line of defense. Clearly, they don't realize that it's one's mind, not the size of her behind, that counts. Well, you can count on me to remind them, every chance I get. Remember that, BIG girls. Make it a mantra. Also remember, there are a few choice names for their frail asses too, like toothpick, beanpole, anorexic, bulimic, wiry, svelte, lean, lithe, emaciated, bony, scrawny, skeletal, malnourished, underfed, hungry, weak, starved, famished, gaunt, slender, trim, sinewy, and tiny—oh, and let's not forget my all-time favorite, skinny bitch. Throw a few of those at them, if you must, because it may be the only way for the BIG and small to peacefully coexist.

Or you may have to do as I finally did and kick skinny bitches to the curb altogether. Get yourself some new girl-friends—F.A.T. ones. Who needs the stress? BIG girls have a simple philosophy about life, and we understand one another. Hungry? Eat. Tired? Take a nap. Hate to jog? Fuck it, just walk. Bottom line, whatever feels good, do it. Send a message that you're cool being a FATTY girl, and folks will begin to see you in a different light.

Speaking of cool: While the majority of skinny women are

a problem, there are a few who're actually, dare I say it, cool. But trust me, they're a rare breed. If you do happen upon one, observe her behavior, and ask a few questions. You may discover she was a CHUBBY child, grew up under the influence of a loving BIG mama, or can honestly see past a few extra pounds to what really matters—the heart. Cool thin ones don't make distinctions. They're generally helpful, friendly, and genuine. They speak first, compliment you on a hot outfit, and indulge right along with us at the all-you-can-eat buffet. If some shit is amiss, cool thin women won't let you leave the house looking crazy. They'll pull us aside and say, "Girl, that red leather bustier looks like its cutting off your circulation, but hey, if you're cool with it, then lets roll." Or, if they see you're about to pass out in a strenuous exercise class, instead of laughing at you, a cool one will whisper, "Girlfriend, fuck this hot Tae-Bo class. Let's go home, eat a salad, and watch the video instead."

Now listen up, BIG girls, because I'm about to offer you a surefire method to measure the level of evil—or coolness—at hand. No need to spend time with the enemy if you don't have to. Especially if you use Mo'Nique's Thin-O-Meter to gauge her behavior—because you can never be too sure. Mo's Thin-O-Meter can truly help you determine what you're dealing with. Because there are a few things to look out for. (1) Attitude: When she enters a room, is she friendly and warm, or standoffish and cold? Most evil ones stand off to the side so they can size up the competition. (2) Appearance: Does she look like a bandage wrapped in spandex from head to toe, or sport lightweight fabrics that blow in the breeze? Skinny bitches will wear some too-tight shit in a minute, and sacrifice comfort for cute. Especially if it'll get them noticed. This may help to determine point number one if you're having trouble.

(3) Conversation: Is her speech peppered with phrases that describe anything BIG or LARGE as bad? Watch that. It's a telling sign. Actions are another important sign. To gauge action, you can use a scale—one to ten, one being a cool thin one and ten standing for the skinniest, foulest bitch you've ever encountered. Does she persuade you to rock something sexy to the club? (That's a cool two.) Tell fucked-up FAT jokes in your presence, then try to play it off and say, "But I'm not talking about you, girl?" (That's an evil eight.) And finally, does she invite you to lunch and then pull up to some soup-and-salad joint and, once you sit down, declare, "Wow, doesn't this look good?" Run, that's an evil ten at work. If you're still having trouble trying to figure it out, never fear, that's why Mo'Nique is here—to get to the bottom of the entire skinny mess.

The issue isn't really whether the BIG and small can get along, but rather, can the skinny see past a few rolls and doubles and handle sharing the spotlight? It's like the difference between handling a Hyundai Sonata and a Porsche 911 Turbo—it's all about how you approach the curves. Some you've got to hug tight, and others you've got to swing real WIDE. Contrary to popular belief, we're not all interested in losing a TON of weight—some of us are happy at 250 pounds, shit, 300 even. We aren't all sad, depressed, and lonely. Most of us have a FULL belly, a FULL refrigerator, and our fill of men.

So, listen up, because here's the deal. If you bought this book expecting a guide to love and acceptance, sorry to disappoint you, because this ain't it. Love and acceptance are qualities you've got to get to on your own. But BIG girls, if you're ready to beat skinny bitches at their own game and take your rightful place in the spotlight, then *Skinny Women Are Evil* is just the book for you. Pay attention and take plenty of notes, because you'll want to be up on the tricks of the small-minded. And if you happen to be a single-digit sister and you're reading this book, consider this your last warning. Either work with us, or we'll be all over you like butter on hot cornbread. OH, IT'S ON! So move over or scoot the fuck out of the way because the FAT is gonna hit the fire and you will get burned. Contrary to popular belief, size really *does* matter. Good things do come in BIG packages—like a BIG house, a BIG car, a BIG bank account, and even a BIG, beautiful woman. After all, inside every skinny bitch is a FAT girl dreaming of—and screaming for—something to eat. Livin' LARGE is more than just a state of mind—it's *the* desired destiny.

With that in mind, sit back and get comfortable, BIG girls. It's time to handle your shit, because it's finally our day. Fuck these skinny bitches. Eat what the fuck you want to eat. In fact, while you're reading this book, go into the kitchen and make yourself a sandwich if the spirit moves you as you read my personal observations on life as a BIG girl in a world aimed at the very small. I'm exposing everything—from the evil tricks of the fashion trade and the games restaurants and health clubs play to the benefits of dating a BIG girl and the trials and tribulations of family and friends—it's all here. So let's get started.

THIN-O-METER

When you really need to know what you're dealing with:

8–10
SKINNY
EVIL ONE

RUN! This is the most evil, back-stabbing, narcissistic woman there is. The SKINNY EVIL ONE has never been F.A.T., never will be F.A.T., and won't even associate with anyone who is. She can't see past a few extra pounds. She'll sell you out. Steal your man. And stab you in the back if she can. After all, it's all about her, and she ain't afraid to let you know it.

4–7
MEDIUM
MAMA

Medium Mama may slip sometimes. But for the most part, she's cool. This woman can roll with the BIG girls and the skinny evil ones too. She's the kind of girl who can do Fatburger on Friday and then tofu on Tuesdays. If a skinny evil one tells a crude FAT joke, MEDIUM MAMA might think it's funny, but she wouldn't dare laugh out loud. Well, not in the presence of her BIG-girl crew, anyway.

0–3
BIG AT
HEART

This is a woman with BIG-girl tendencies. She may have been THICK, may have a mother, grandmother, or sister on the THICK side, or may secretly want to be THICK. The BIG AT HEART sister identifies with BIG-girl ways. She's a cool thin one who loves a damn good buffet every now and then. You'll never hear her say, "Girl, you're too fat to wear that."

You're Probably a Skinny Evil One If . . .

* You've ever gone out with three of your girlfriends and split a salad four ways.

* You've ever offered everyone in the room dessert except the F.A.T. girl.

* You've ever said, "But you have such a pretty face."

* You've never even been to a Lane Bryant store.

* You've never worn pants with an elastic waistband.

* You go into the store, and the size zero is too big.

* You shop all day without taking a lunch break.

* You order soup at Sizzler.

* You spend the entire day working out at the gym.

* You ask for everything on the side at restaurants.

* During sex you scream, Stop, that hurts! and you're on top.

* You can make it from one gate to the other at Chicago's O'Hare in less than ten minutes.

* You're full from the airplane peanuts.

* A good wind will knock you over.

* You can slip through the shoulder harness on a roller coaster.

* Your favorite store is Gap Kids—and you're thirty-five.

* You pull out a food scale in a restaurant and weigh your food.

* You count carbs at a health-food restaurant.

* You order the McSalad/McSoup Combo at McDonald's and don't Supersize it.

* None of your clothes cover your belly button.

* Someone asks you a good place to eat, and you can't think of any.

* You think Jenny Craig is a talk-show host.

* Your only job is to look good for your man.

* You've ever ordered like this: "I'll have the Cobb salad, but no egg, no avocado, no bacon, no bleu cheese, no tomatoes, and the dressing on the side, please."

Phrases That'll Let You Know She's Probably Evil

* Does this make me look fat?

* I'm not hungry. I ate yesterday.

* Can I get this in a size zero?

* You ate the whole thing?

* Two bites and it's, "I'm stuffed."

* How did she get him?

* How BIG is that?

* Are you really going to wear that?

* More than a mouthful is a waste.

* Are you pregnant? With twins?

* We only carry that in up to a size twelve.

* Exactly how BIG are you?

* Can I move my seat, please?

* She must be dating Stevie Wonder.

* Do you have a glandular problem?

* It must be because she's got money.

Phrases That'll Let You Know She May Be Cool

* Let's go over to the new Hometown Buffet.

* I brought a dozen Krispy Kremes for you, too.

* Girl, you better work that tight dress. It looks sexy on you.

* I wish I had a bootie like that.

* I wish I had some boobs like that.

* You wanna hit the food court first?

* Let's just get a limo instead.

* Forget Billy Blanks. Let's just go home.

* He's got a fine cousin.

* Is it me, or are these damn airplane seats tight?

* Let me get the Cobb salad with extra bacon bits, extra bleu cheese, and extra dressing on the side, oh, and some extra bread and butter too.

* Girl, let's get dessert.

Important Years in Big-Girl History

1904—**Mary McCleod Bethune** founds Bethune Cookman College, formerly Daytona Literary and Industrial School for Training Negro Girls.

1917—Hair-care pioneer **Madam C. J. Walker** organizes the first Madam C. J. Walker Hair Culturists Union convention in Philadelphia.

1940—**Hattie McDaniel** wins Best Supporting Actress for *Gone with the Wind* at the Oscars.

1950—**Ella Baker** helps create the Southern Christian Leadership Conference (SCLC).

1951—**Louise Beavers** stars in *Beulah*, the first sitcom to feature a black person in the title role.

1964—Political activist **Fannie Lou Hamer** helps to form the Mississippi Freedom Democratic Party (MFDP). She is famous for her words, "I'm sick and tired of being sick and tired."

1970—**Maya Angelou's** autobiographical work *I Know Why the Caged Bird Sings* becomes a best-seller.

1974—Singer **Mama Cass Elliot** allegedly dies after choking on a ham sandwich. The real cause of death was a heart attack.

1976—**Barbara Jordan** becomes the first woman and first African American to give the keynote speech at the Democratic National Convention.

1986—The *Oprah Winfrey* Show debuts.

1986—**Dorothy Height** organizes the Black Family Reunion Celebration to reinforce traditional values of the black family.

1988—**Oprah** gains weight back and then really BLOWS UP—in her career, that is.

1993—**Queen Latifah** debuts in the hit comedy *Living Single*.
Ricki Lake's show debuts.

1995—**Loretta Devine** gets her man in *Waiting to Exhale*.

1997—**Camryn Manheim** joins the cast of *The Practice*.

1999—**Mo'Nique** lands her sitcom *The Parkers*.

2001—**Mo'Nique** wins NAACP award for Outstanding Actress in a Comedy Series.

2002—Full-figured supermodel **Emme** launches the full-figured Emme doll.

Lane Bryant kicks off Fashion Week in New York City.

Mo'Nique becomes the first female host of *Showtime at the Apollo*.

Marissa Jaret Winouker is the toast of Broadway in *Hairspray*.

My Big Fat Greek Wedding remains in the top-five spot at the box office for weeks.

Mo'Nique wins the NAACP award for Outstanding Actress in a Comedy Series, again.

Grace, a magazine dedicated to full-figured women, debuts.

TWO

Friends and Family

DON'T YOU JUST LOVE 'EM?

I'M THE BIGGEST member of my family—the entire family. At birth, I came bouncing into the world weighing a healthy nine pounds, twelve ounces. And when my parents brought me home from the hospital, relatives took one look and said, "Are you sure she's yours?" I was. But the question was fair, because my mom, Miss Alice, as she's affectionately known, is five-three, and my father is nearly six feet, and both of them are slim people.

So are my older brothers, Gerald and Steve, and my sister, Millicent. Though I'm the baby of the bunch, that didn't mean a thing, because like most siblings, we fought like cats and dogs. But we'll get to that later. What I can say is that mine was a typical middle-class upbringing, filled with love. They say a girl's father is the first man she'll ever love, and mine—bless his heart—is the best. My father worked as a prison guard at Patuxent Correctional Institute in Jessup, Maryland, for thirty years, and my mom retired from a career

as a quality control manager for Westinghouse. As the bread-
winner, my father didn't have much time for extracurricular
activities, but he did instill a sense of strength in all four of his
children and told me, from the time I could understand
words, that I was the prettiest girl in the world. Even now,
after thirty-five years, he still calls me the prettiest girl in the
world. So I never went through that phase in life where I felt
like something was wrong with me. He always made my sister
and me feel special and fought anyone who tried to hurt his
baby girls. With that kind of love and reinforcement, I was
able to eventually go out into the world and fight my own battles, and it came in handy around the age of five on the playground at school. That's probably about when I realized I
wasn't like all the other kids. I was BIGGER. Fighting BIG
battles as a kid was tough, but when it all got to be too much
for one BIG little girl to handle, thank goodness I could
always run home to the loving arms of family. My mom was—
and still is—an incredible mom. How she was able to work a
full-time job and still find the time and energy to deal with
four small children, I don't know, but she always involved us in
activities that would make us well rounded. There was charm
school, but I was always about keepin' it real, so that didn't last
long. There were singing lessons, but I couldn't carry a note,
so there was no need to waste hard-earned dollars. When I
wrote a play called *The Missing Dog* and held nightly performances in the living room, she was there. She never missed a
school play, like the one in the tenth grade when I was cast as
background.

When I wasn't performing my nightly living-room act, or
expressing some other form of talent, I was bugging my sister
Millicent in our bedroom. Three years my senior, Millicent
was always a glamour puss. Her hair was perfect. Her figure

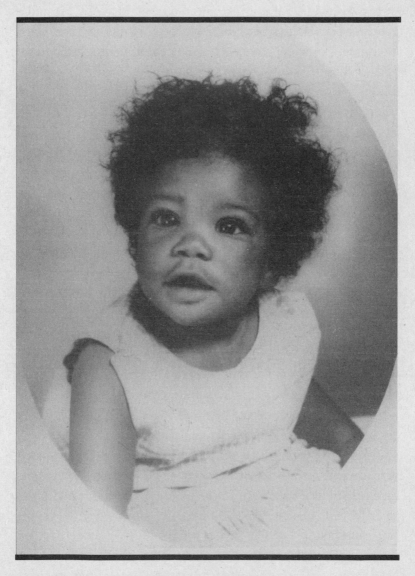

Me, six months. The hair. The eyes. The smile.
Even as a baby, I was a star.

was, too. And she always sported the latest fashions with flair. But to Millicent, I was a FAT pig. So how do a FAT pig and a glamour puss share a bedroom? By fighting like cats and dogs, of course. For a few years we hated each other, and though we had to share a room, that was about all we had in common. Though I couldn't fit her clothes, that didn't stop me from trying to squeeze into her stockings, or anything else I could get my hands on, and getting a beat-down for it. The law of the house was no fighting or name-calling, but we broke that law regularly, especially since I was a tattletale. Whenever her friends came over to visit, or called, I'd eavesdrop on her conversations, and I made it my duty to inform our parents what their oldest daughter was up to, especially since she refused to let me tag along. That's right. I was the family informant. One particular time, she was plotting an escape and I got wind of it, so I told on her. The Battle Royale was on. The fight started in the bathroom and went all the way into the bedroom, where we proceeded to kill each other. Eventually my father came in and broke us up, but by that time I had scratched her in the face, and she had punched me in the stomach. Thank goodness it was a BIG stomach, and I could take a punch. And it was hard to separate us, because I was HEAVY. One time my mother went to pick me up and damn near threw her back out. Looking back on those years, it's incredible how much hatred went on in that little room. It wasn't until years later that I discovered we were really jealous of one another. I was an independent spirit, and though she always wanted to be, Millicent actually relied on the wrong folks to make it. I, on the other hand, wanted to wear the cute clothes and shoes and have the friends my sister had, at least the good ones, anyway.

When he was twenty-one, the last thing my oldest brother, Gerald, wanted to do was baby-sit his bratty little sisters and brother. He was grown and didn't hesitate to remind us of that fact. So asking him to give up a Saturday night was like asking a skinny bitch to eat—it ain't happening. But my mother promptly put a dent in his plans by making him stay home and taking the car. Stranded in the house, he punished us for making him miss one of the hottest parties by chasing around the house, and when he caught us, it was on. The three of us couldn't wait to report the events of the evening to our parents the moment they got home. Steve, Millicent, and I were getting our story together, but before they got home, Gerald caught me in the hallway. He figured if it was two against two, maybe he'd get away, so he bribed me not to tell. The reward—a Snickers candy bar. When my parents got home, Steve and Millicent were on their coattails, but I was hiding out with my candy bar. When my parents asked me what happened, I put on an Oscar-worthy performance and acted as if Steve and Millicent were crazy. Needless to say, Gerald won that one. But it was Steve who cut me deep when he called me a FAT pig. It was a Saturday night, and he was getting dressed for a date, but my mother told him that if he wanted to use the car, he'd have to drop me off at a friend's house. He was pissed because it was out of his way. I was just happy to be out on a Saturday night with my BIG brother. When he was ready to go, I heard him utter under his breath, "Come on, you FAT pig." Of course, I told, but my mother didn't hear it, so he got away. He knew if Miss Alice heard that one, he would've been chillin' at the house, too. And the last thing he wanted was to get caught in the house on a Saturday night. After all, he had a reputation to protect.

So did my mother. Miss Alice didn't play. She was a swinger. And I'm not talking in the sexual sense. If you disobeyed, she'd knock you upside the head, and it could happen

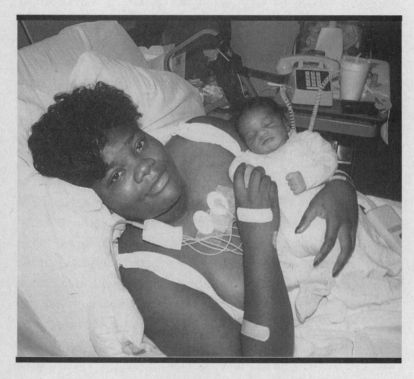

I was worn the hell out! But the look on my baby boy Shalon's
face made it all worth it.

anytime and anywhere. Like the time she caught me off guard in a department store. Now, you know how kids play. I was running around like a wild woman, and my mother couldn't shop, so she told me to go sit with Gerald. But I got smart and told her, "You go sit with Gerald." When I woke up, I was on top of the mannequins. I'm not sure how many miles per hour her hand flew or when her fist connected with my head. Once I managed to make it up from the floor, I found a chair, sat my smart ass down, and didn't move an inch until she said so. Another time, Millicent and I were jumping around the house while Mom was trying to do the laundry. We kept flipping into the basket. She was so frustrated that she tied us to the refrigerator with a rope until she finished the laundry. Now today, that's considered child abuse, but back in the day, that was the only way a tired woman with four kids could get any work done around the house. We sat there laughing and talking like it was nothing. Those were the good old days. Even though I bugged the hell out of my sister, as we got older, I became less dependent on her. Unfortunately, we drifted apart. I'm sure Millicent enjoyed our fights as much as I did. Years later, our fight would take a much different turn.

By the time she was sixteen, there was nothing sweet about Millicent's activities. She started to drink, smoke, and run with a fast crowd. Like a lot of kids her age, Millicent thought she was slick enough not to get caught up, and she began stealing money from the family. Now, to a thirteen-year-old, forty dollars was a lot of money. So, when twenty of the forty dollars I had on the dresser came up missing, it was time for a sisterly powwow, or knockout. Even back then, there were three things you didn't mess with—my mama, my food, and my money, and not necessarily in that order. When I confronted

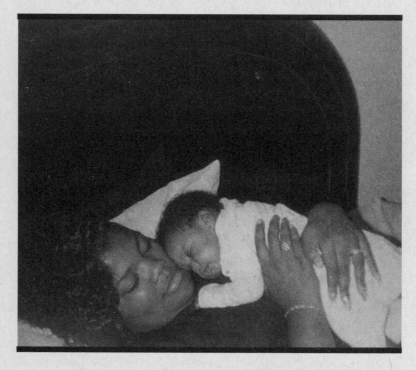

I love babies. This is me with my niece Jasmine taking a nap.

her, she denied it, but I knew what she was up to. When I told on her, my mother, who was also in denial, made up excuses for her, like maybe it fell behind the dresser, or, Are you sure you didn't spend it? "Oh, it got spent all right, but not by me," I told her. After a while, things went from bad to worse. I knew Millicent was in trouble when she began to nod off while singing "Rock a Bye Baby" to her baby girl. My mother said, "Wow, she's just really, really tired." I said, "No, Ma, she's really, really high." My family had a hard time acknowledging that their oldest daughter was on drugs, especially since Millicent had always been a drop-dead gorgeous girl. It hurt me, too. I could see my sister was ruining her life. It got so bad that she didn't care about her appearance. She was always on edge, and it was taking a toll on our mother. As much as it hurt, I had to practice tough love and told her, "I cannot be a part of your life until you get clean." It took some time, but she eventually checked herself into rehab and, with support from the entire family, got through one of the toughest periods of her life. She's been clean for ten years and is once again the BIG sister I always knew and loved.

Like most little girls, I loved dealing with my daddy. He had a way of making you see things from a totally different perspective—his. By the time I was old enough to drive, I just had to have the new 1989 Ford Festiva, and I expected him to cosign so I could get it. Wrong. His philosophy was, That's your dream, not mine. If you want it, you've got to earn it yourself. That's Steven Imes Jr. for you. He knew how to dash a dream, but in actuality he was helping me create my own. At the time I was working as a customer service representative for Washington Express, a courier service in Baltimore. It took months, but eventually I saved enough money to put down $500, and baby, I loved that car. It may have only had an

AM stereo, but it was mine, and there was no eating in the car—well, for the first two weeks, anyway. I didn't realize it at the time but after dealing with inmates for thirty years, he knew how to get his point across without so much as an argument. It's no surprise that after retiring, he went back to school, earned a degree in clinical psychology, and embarked on a second career. Daddy's rationale, that I take full responsibility for buying my own car, didn't fall on deaf ears. Years later, when I purchased my first Mercedes-Benz 500 SL, I picked him up to go for a spin, he saw how much I cherished that car and said, "See, Nique, how much more you appreciate things when you get them on your own. You wouldn't know the feeling of pride if I'd have bought it for you." Point well taken. My father taught me many lessons.

Like, at the age of seven, that there was no Santa Claus. He was supposed to spend Christmas Eve assembling all the toys so that Christmas morning when we woke up, we could run downstairs and tear into our gifts. My mother had bought me a kitchen set, that was supposed to have real running water. My father was clearly feeling the holiday spirit and sipping a few, too, because he and my mother got into an argument when he told her he planned to put my kitchen set together on Christmas Day. She should have let him. Instead she insisted, "No, Steve. When Nique wakes up, she's got to see the water running." So, drunk as a skunk, he attempted to put it together. The next day not only did the water not run, but all of the gifts he attempted to assemble were so messed up we spent the entire day reassembling everything. It never occurred to me that we didn't have a chimney until I caught them sneaking gifts upstairs into a spare room. In my seven-year-old mind, Santa brought the chimney and gifts with him, and then took the chimney when he was done. I never put it together, and my father never put together another Christmas gift.

There was also a summer trip to Kings Dominion in Virginia. Vibrating beds had just come out, and I was intrigued. So my father gave me a roll of quarters, and I lay on my stomach in the bed, put every single one of them into the slot, and let the bed do its thing. It made my stomach wiggle and made me laugh, uncontrollably. Oh, did I mention the entire family was in one room? My mom and dad were in one bed, and Millicent, Stevie, and I were in another. Everyone was aggravated because every time they'd doze off, I'd start the bed up again. The next day, penniless, I begged my father for some more money, but he told me all my money was back in the room, in the bed. That trip was one of the most memorable—and for me the most broke—family vacations I ever had.

We had a rather large extended family, and playing with my cousins was always fun, but when it came to aunts, my mother's sister was a real drama queen. If there was a problem, she'd blow it way out of proportion and flip on me in a minute. For some reason, members of our extended family thought that we thought we were better. There was one time we were sitting on my aunt's front steps, and my cousin was braiding my hair. We heard a commotion and spotted my uncle coming up the street. It was obvious he'd had a little too much to drink, and some of the neighborhood kids were picking on him, so of course I stood up and tried to come to his rescue. "Y'all better leave my uncle alone!" I shouted. My aunt heard the commotion and came outside to see what was going on. But when she got to the door, instead of helping her husband out, she told me to shut up. "Ma'am?" I said, surprised. "Shut up before I hit you in the mouth," she said. I

Whenever I can, I love to take time to hang with my little boyfriend, Shalon. This is one of our family vacations in the Bahamas.
Isn't he handsome?

couldn't believe she was yelling at me after I was trying to take up for her drunk husband. But she was serious. "You won't hit me," I told her, "because I'll hit you right back." Pissed, I got up from the stoop and attempted to march my BIG ass home with half of my hair plaited and the other half wild as hell. But we lived too far, and it was too close to dinner, so I turned around and came back. Though I was a fun-loving little girl, for some reason I rubbed this aunt the wrong way. Especially when it came to her cooking. Now, growing up, my mother never cooked grits because my father didn't like them. So it wasn't until I was about eight years old and staying at my aunt's house that I tasted *the* breakfast staple of black—and some white—households. I came down to the table on Sunday morning, sat down, and noticed something that looked like mashed potatoes. So I asked my aunt, "Why are we eating mashed potatoes for breakfast?" Baby, she was insulted. "I'm so sorry we don't have pancakes and eggs, and bacon and sausage, like you do over at your house. All we've got here is grits, girl. So take it or leave it." I decided to leave it, and her house, too. It wasn't until a few years later that I finally figured out the problem—jealousy. When my father and mother married, he moved her away to the suburbs. And my mother was able to keep her husband. But my aunt, well, let's just say I had a different uncle every couple of years. So anytime she got a chance to stick it to us, she did. And every chance I could get smart with her, I did. The funniest thing about this entire situation was that my mother told me that growing up, I looked just like her. Once my aunt even told my mother, "That Mo'Nique is too loud and boisterous, and that other one will probably be pregnant before you know it." After I made it to Hollywood—by being loud and boisterous—this same aunt started to brag to anybody who would listen about how close we were and how I spent my early years eating grits at her house. But to this day, she's never once picked up the phone and called to say, Baby, I'm proud of you. She may not have had much to give, but growing up, all she needed to give was love and support. Maybe she got her meanness from her mama.

Most kids love to visit grandparents, but not me. As much as I loved my maternal grandmother, looking back, I don't think she liked me very much. Or, if she did, she had a strange way of showing it. She could be loving if she wanted to be, but she could also be a very strict, no-nonsense woman who didn't hesitate to speak her mind. No matter how hard I tried I just couldn't seem to get on her good side. In her eyes, I was a BIG monster. If you don't believe it, listen to what she did to me when I was eighteen. Like most teenagers, boys were an important part of life, but throw an old grandmother into the mix and things had a way of going horribly awry.

One day, a family friend was over her house and he kept staring at me. After a while, he finally got up the nerve to tell me how pretty he thought I was. Now, this did wonders for my burgeoning self-esteem. But, before I could bask in the compliment, my grandmother blurted out, "She used to be very pretty. Then she just blew up. I don't know what's wrong with her." The boy was shocked and I wanted to go some-where and crawl under a rock. My own grandmother sold me out. But, that wasn't the end of it. On another occasion, she caught me eating ice and told me, in a roomful of people, not to let her catch me eating ice again because it would make me FATTER than I already was. I said to myself, "Ain't this a bitch. Ice is FATTENING." My mother's response, when I came home crying was, "Oh, Mo'Nique, they're just jokes." But my father's answer was to cuss folks out. Sadly, my grandmother passed during the first season of the show. Though I never had an opportunity to ask her why she treated me so badly, the last time we talked, she said, "You know, Baby, when you moved away, you took all of my sunshine." I was shocked to know that she cared enough to miss me. I guess you never know the role you play in someone's life, or the effect they'll have on yours. Though she said some hurtful things, I thank God for a forgiving heart and for the opportunity to spend time with her before she passed away. I'm sure in her own special way she was trying to let me know how much she loved me. A hug would have been nice.

Nice is definitely the word to describe my paternal grandmother, Mimmi. She was the fun one. Whenever we went to her house, she had all the food, gifts, and toys any kid could hope for. Mimmi was a generous spirit and it was always a delight to stay at her house, as we often did. Along with our grandfather, BIG Daddy, who was a cool dude, too, and would do anything for you, we always looked forward to a visit. In Mimmi's eyes, I was the greatest thing since sliced bread, and she treated all of us like gold. She still lives in Baltimore and watches the show every week, and brags to her friends about her baby girl who went out to California and made it BIG.

You know the song by Whodini, "Friends?" It was hot back in the day, and I'm fortunate to have a tight crew of girlfriends who have remained in my life. Charisse, or "Pooh" as we called her, and I met in the second grade at Woodmoor Elementary School. She was all of about a size zero, and prissy as could be, but she was one of the cool thin ones. And the child could fight her ass off. I've got a lot of mouth, but when it comes to backing up the talk, I'm a lover, not a fighter. So, for all the talking I did, Charisse was the enforcer. Then there was Michelle, who was a smaller version of me. In fact, folks thought we were sisters. Michelle was one of the sweetest people you'll ever meet. If she was your girl, she had your back to the end, but there's no two ways about it, Michelle was a roughneck, plain and simple. Girlfriend could definitely walk the walk and back up any tough talk. She loved to fight, too. In fact, Michelle loved it so much she's been locked up for it. Yolanda was THICK, like me. I liked to call her the brains of the group. She was sensible, levelheaded, and quiet. Yolanda wasn't swinging at all. Lisa started out a BIG girl, but lost about sixty pounds and nearly got her BIG-girl card revoked. For a moment she teetered on the edge of being a cool thin one and a skinny evil bitch, but all it took was a couple of hamburgers to solve Lisa's problem.

The cool thing about our clique was that everyone knew her place in the friendship. I was the one who could get whatever you needed done. Any kind of fun stuff, they knew to call me. Charisse had a car. Michelle had everybody's back. If there was some lick you wanted to pull and didn't want the parental figures to know what was up, Lisa's house was the said destination. And Yolanda was the homework whiz. At all the high school basketball and football games, my girls and I screamed, cheered, and sang over the top of the skinny cheerleaders, and literally ran the school. But when you're running things, there are always those who will try to test you.

Anyone who knows me knows that I'm always about fairness. Righting wrongs. Standing up for the underdog. But that line of thinking almost got me a beat-down by seven girls when a rumor started that one of my good guy friends had gotten a girl pregnant. Now, if you're going to spread a rumor, don't tell me the truth, because Mo'Nique will tell it. The girl told me it really wasn't my friend's baby, but she never planned to tell my poor friend, so I did—after all, it was

My sister Millicent, my dad, my mom Miss Alice, me,
and my sister-in-law Kelly.

the right thing to do. But it pissed her off, so she and her crew were on the lookout and found me in a deserted hallway on my way to class. Even back then, I dressed like I had a nine-to-five job, so when they caught up with me, in my gray skirt suit, black pumps, and carrying a briefcase, I wasn't about to fight. They surrounded me and asked why I told the boy it wasn't his baby. Now, I'm a scaredy-cat, so I tried to reason with them first. "Look," I said. "I don't have time for this foolishness." They weren't buying my act and proceeded to close in. Ordinarily, my crew would have handled it, but we had split up. With each step, I was becoming more and more frightened. And I was on the verge of tears, when I happened to look up and notice Michelle rounding the corner. I don't know how she found me, but I was glad to see her. So I did the only thing I could do. I started talking shit because help was on the way. As those bullies were closing in for the kill, Michelle swooped into the middle of the madness and got in the BIGGEST one's face. "What the hell is going on here?" she asked. And trust me, they didn't want any of Michelle. "Oh, nothing," the ringleader said as she backed it up. "We were just talking to Mo'Nique." "Well, y'all ain't gonna talk to her right now, so move it," Michelle yelled. "Yeah," I added, "move it." I strolled away confidently, but after that scrap, Michelle looked at me and said, " 'Nique, I told you that fucking mouth was going to get you in trouble. Let's go."

Sophomore year, Charisse had to set it off. And she had the tendency to shake a lot, but that didn't stop her from handling beef whenever it came her way. One day a girl confronted her because she'd heard that Charisse called her out of her name, and Charisse confirmed that she did indeed call the girl ugly. The girl was determined to show Charisse just how bad an ugly girl could beat her up, so she challenged her to a fight after school. Of course, Michelle was in, and the rest of us were expected to show up for moral support. As soon as the bell rang, the crew was getting together. It was understood that if one of us fought, the whole clique was expected to help out. Now, I was trying to find some kind of way to get out of it. As we were headed to the match, I was trying to reason with them. "Now, y'all know we can't be fightin'," I said. But they weren't trying to hear it. These were my girls, and it was all for one and one for all. I realized there was no way out. They expected me to scrap. But, I was one of those hit-'em-and-run kind of girls. Shit, I couldn't get caught in the pileup, so when Charisse cold-cocked her and Michelle drop-kicked the girl, I ran in, knocked her in the head once, and ran out. Shit, a queen shouldn't swing, and I wasn't trying to explain to my mother and father that I got suspended from school for fighting someone else's battle.

But getting people straight seemed to be a never-ending quest with my crew. By senior year, the rule of the school was, if you were caught fighting, it was an automatic suspension. This time around, a girl had some friends from New York come to town and rob Michelle's brother. Now this damn near started a riot. Though she didn't do it, this girl was there when the deed went down, so Michelle was on the hunt, and when she found her, she let her know in no uncertain terms that she could expect an ass-whipping on GP—general principle. Once again, I'm the punk of the group, and I'm trying my damnedest to get out of this melee. But Michelle was serious. She told the girl that she was going to do it, and she planned to, with our help, of course. So the day of the BIG fight, I'm there with my girls getting the licks in. By the time the dust cleared, my bra strap had been torn off and my shirt had been ripped to shreds, but baby, my hair never moved. I

My class picture from third grade. That's me, third from the left,
top row, and Charisse, fourth from the right in the middle row.

may have had to fight, but damn it, I was gonna look cute doin' it.

After fighting for everyone else, it was finally my time. But my fight was equivalent to a Mike Tyson-Evander Holyfield heavyweight boxing match between me and a girl named BIG Sam. We were in the same math class, and BIG Sam was a THICK sister with a BIG bush. One day I came into class, and she was sitting in my seat. I asked her to move several times, but she said, "I ain't going nowhere." Now, that was enough to scare the hell out of me. They didn't call her BIG Sam for nothing. This girl had a face only a mother could love. So I found another seat—after I told on her, of course. I thought it was squashed until BIG Sam walked by and kicked my chair with her BIG size tens. I thought to myself, Lord, don't let me have to fight this FAT girl. But there was no getting around it. BIG Sam continued to terrorize me. So I recruited Michelle. " 'Chelle," I said, scared as usual. "Can you get her because she done kicked up on my chair?" That's all Michelle needed to hear. That afternoon, she caught Sam in the locker room and handled it. I, of course, did my usual one hit and got the hell out. Looking back now, it's a wonder I made it out alive, especially since I was the woman voted most popular and best dressed in high school.

After high school, we all went our separate ways, but we stayed in touch, and the friendship continued. Michelle now owns her own party-planning business in Baltimore; Lisa works for the National Security Agency in the city; Yolanda is a social worker in Ohio; and sadly, my beautiful friend Charisse passed away in October 2002 after a lengthy illness. I'm so grateful to have spoken with her at length the Saturday before she passed. Though she's gone, the bond we shared is eternal, and I'm confident she's in a better place.

No bond, perhaps, is deeper than the one I share with my brother, Steve. While I was growing up, he was my protector, and I was his most loyal servant. When he got a newspaper route and put on his coat and shoes to throw papers, I was right there alongside him, putting on my little boots and coat to throw papers, too. He combed my hair, and if anyone talked badly about his baby sister, Stevie would knock 'em. When nobody else would, Stevie would sit in the living room and endure my horrible plays, and always listened to my childhood rants about wanting to be a star someday. Though he probably thought I was crazy, my brother never dashed my dreams or laughed when I told him I couldn't wait for the day when complete strangers would stare at me in restaurants.

Of course, it took a while to figure out how to make that happen, and along the way I did everything to get there. First it was music lessons. When I landed an audition for a performing arts school in New York, my mother, Stevie, and I got into the car and headed to New York for what would potentially be my BIG break. I had my repertoire together. When they called my name, my mom and Stevie gave me the once-over, fixed my dress, and marched me in there to dazzle 'em. And though they weren't feeling my remix of "The Sun Will Come Out Tomorrow," from the musical *Annie*, that didn't stop Miss Alice and Steve from cheering me on from the back of the room, anyway, like I was Miss Jennifer Holiday. From there, it was ballet lessons, but I was on the CHUBBY side, and my tutu was too, too BIG. By high school, I joined the debate team or anything else to make people say, "I want to be with Mo'Nique," though my mission in life didn't become clear until much later. There were many more endeavors, like a stint as a phone-sex operator—actually, I trained the girls—a gig as a full-figured model for Just Us Plus Modeling Agency, and, in high school, a job at

Me and my mom, Miss Alice.
She gets a paycheck just for simply being the best mom in the world.

Popeye's. There was also a stint at Hutzler's department store, and work as a customer service representative at MCI, before I finally found my calling—comedy.

I can honestly say that I owe my stand-up success to my brother's failure at it. Back in 1988, Steve was a frustrated FBI computer programmer, moonlighting as a stand-up comic. One night he'd had a few too many drinks and let his friends convince him that he was funnier than he really was. He got up onstage and told what was probably the corniest joke in history. It went a little something like this: A football team was in the locker room, getting pumped up for the BIG game. The coach was trying to get his team motivated and told them, Okay, I want you guys to go out there and get ferocious. One of the players raised his hand and said, Okay, coach, what number is he? You probably aren't laughing, and neither was anyone in the room that night. Needless to say, that corny shit got the promoters to pull the plug and turn the lights off on my poor brother right in the middle of his routine. He got booed so badly that he retired from comedy that night. That's right. That was the end of Steve's comedy career—and the beginning of mine. We've always been competitive, so when I got wind of the fact that he stunk up the place, I teased him unmercifully. Steve was so frustrated that he dared me to get up onstage and try my hand at comedy. Never one to back away from a challenge, I went to the same club he had bombed at the week before.

Burke's was a local hot spot that had dancing downstairs and comedy upstairs. It was an open-mike night the night we showed up, and the place was packed. I signed up, studied other people's routines, and waited my turn, nervous as could be. When they finally called my name, I took to the stage and opened with, "y'all give it up for my FAT ass. . . ." The crowd roared with laughter as I proceeded to do seven minutes of jokes about a subject I was all too familiar with—life as a BIG girl. That night, I received my first standing ovation and at that moment found my calling. A star was born on that stage—well, in my mind, anyway. Afterward, someone came up and asked Steve who my manager was. They wanted to hire me to emcee a hair show and pay me twenty-five dollars. Steve immediately took the ball and ran with it, negotiating an additional five dollars for gas money. That night my brother became my manager.

And what a career we've shared. Steve remembered my desire to have the world know me and went to work to make it happen. When I wanted to be fabulous like Ginger on *Gilligan's Island*, he got me new clothes and shoes for my gigs, and when I pointed to Louise "Weezie" Jefferson from *The Jeffersons* as *the* black woman I wanted to emulate, my brother said, In time, my child, in time. Getting there was no easy task. Steve booked me to perform for the KKK, had me on a whirlwind three-city tour, and had me play venues so small it was just me, the cleanup guy, and the bartender. Along the way he's made some bad decisions, but he's also taken me to heights I only dreamed of, and our bond only deepened when my career began to really take off.

One of our earliest endeavors was Mo'Nique's Comedy Club. It was 1990, and I was back in Baltimore with my son after a failed marriage. Opening that club was like a dream come true; after we persuaded the owner of a Persian restaurant to let us host comedy there a couple of nights a week, he eventually sold us the place. We took it over, debt and all, and turned it into a full-fledged comedy club. On the surface, it looked beautiful, but in reality the place was a safety hazard. We spent so much money purchasing it that we couldn't afford to fix it up. The kitchen wasn't always operable—especially with the gaping hole in the floor and constant water

See, not all skinny women are evil.
This is one of the last pictures of Charisse and me on a trip to the
Bahamas. Charisse was one of the cool ones.

leaks. The ice machine stayed on the blink, so drinks were served warm most times, and let's just say the food wouldn't win any culinary awards. How we stayed open for three years without getting cited for health-code violations is still a mystery. It didn't take long for Mo'Nique's to become one of Baltimore's premiere comedy venues. It was truly a family affair. Miss Alice sold tickets at the door, Steve was the club manager, Millicent, who was a systems analyst at AT&T at the time, spread the word to coworkers, and Gerald, a car salesman, handed out flyers at work. By then my routine was catching on, and folks were talking about the FAT girl at the comedy club doing stand-up.

By 1993 we had gotten too BIG for Baltimore. Steve had booked me at every venue in town, helped me open my own comedy club, and negotiated appearances on all of the hot comedy shows at the time: *Showtime at the Apollo* and HBO's shows *Def Comedy Jam* and *Snaps*. When it was time to take my career to the next level, our relationship was tested when a well-known New York manager called with an offer. Finally, the break we had both been waiting for. We packed up the car and drove from Baltimore to New York to meet with this man, who promised everything from a television sitcom deal to feature films, endorsements, comedy tours, and any other thing my heart desired. It all sounded too good to be true. We were ready to sign on the dotted line until Steve inquired about the possibility of comanagement. Indignant, the man flatly refused. Steve was disappointed, but it sounded like such a wonderful opportunity, he was willing to step aside so this BIG-time manager could sign me. However, it didn't sit well with my spirit. Steve and I had been together from the beginning, and if we were going to make it, then we had to make it together. After a few days, I called the manager back and told

him if he didn't take Steve, then he didn't get me. He had the
gall to tell me that no one would respect Steve as my brother
and manager in this business. Now, that's where he was
wrong. What I needed was someone who cared about me as
more than a client. It only made sense that I share this journey
with the one man who had been there from the start and had
been a fan of my earlier living-room performances—my
brother. Shortly after that meeting, Steve began to show his
mettle. We received a call from Don Wiener, the executive
producer of *Showtime at the Apollo*. He was developing a talk
show with four women and wanted me to be a cohost. We
shot the pilot, but as things go in Hollywood, it never got
picked up. Steve worked hard to land something else, and it
was about a year later that we attended the Just for Laughs
Comedy Festival in Montreal. This is *the* premier showcase
for emerging comics to perform for sold-out crowds while
attempting to woo industry bigwigs. It's also the place where
careers are made and deals are inked annually, and a place that
unites talent with agents, management, and most notably,
high-profile TV development executives. In addition to on-
the-spot deals, the festival has helped folks get discovered. I
arrived in Canada with a talk show in the works, and left with
talk of a proposed sitcom. In no time, we were flown out to
L.A. to meet with several network executives and show run-
ners. Suzie Unger, an executive at Disney at the time, liked my
pilot. When she moved into agenting, she asked me to wait
and sign with her at the William Morris Agency. Once she was
there, Suzie placed copies of my head shot everywhere and
persuaded the top brass to sign me on as a client. They did.
Suzie worked in the daytime talk division, and after I had
secured several talk-show pilots without success, my tape fell
into the hands of Larry Lyttle, president of Big Ticket

Steve, looking like a million dollars, in a ten-dollar suit.

Television. Larry took one look at my tape and said, "She's not a talk-show host, she's a sitcom star. If she can act, I'll give her a show." By five that evening the deal for *The Parkers* was sealed, and within a month we were shooting the pilot.

I'm certain it's through the grace of God and Steve's hard work that we landed that deal, and I know it's no accident that Big Ticket is the company that put a BIG girl on television. Despite the fact that Steve was told he'd never make it in this town because he's not a Hollywood player, he's done a damn good job with my career. And I'm not just saying that because he's my brother. He knows how to make a star. I've toured all over America, Africa, and Japan. And when Walter Latham, producer of the successful Kings of Comedy tour that featured Steve Harvey, Cedric the Entertainer, Bernie Mac, and D. L. Hughley, decided to put together a Queens of Comedy tour, Steve was instrumental in negotiating that deal—with me as headliner. He knew I always wanted to be a movie star, and shortly after the comedy tour was over, my brother secured three film deals. Like I said, Steve knows his stuff, and I love him for it. But he also knows how to work my damn nerves. I've fired him at least twenty-five times, usually when we fail to see eye to eye on my career, but the bottom line is that I believe in him and he believes in me.

Apparently, that crazy New York manager finally believed too, because at the end of 1998, when we shot the pilot for the show, this fool had the nerve to show up on the set, laughing and shooting the breeze like nothing ever happened. I was pissed, but Steve played along with his shucking and jiving for a while. It didn't take him long to close in for the kill, and by the end of the evening, he made his bid to Steve about the possibility of comanagement. And if that weren't enough of an insult, he had the audacity to tell Steve to draw up a proposal detailing what he

Me and Millicent.

could bring to the table. Now, I was ready to fight, because I didn't think he should have been there in the first place, but Steve was cool. He knew he had the upper hand. His response: Why don't you send us a proposal, stating how your services will benefit us? Needless to say, we never heard from that joker again.

Steve's favorite phrase is, "Mo'Nique, trust me." I'm happy to say that I do value his opinion and know he would never steer me wrong. It's truly a blessing to have an opportunity to do what I love and have someone in my corner who genuinely cares about me. And it's amazing when I really stop to think about how the Lord puts people in our lives for a reason. When we arrived in Los Angeles, we knew no one, but now I have a tight circle of friends who are just like family. I had no idea after meeting *Parkers* creators Sara Finney-Johnson, Ralph Farquhar, and Vida Spears that I would be working with three of the most talented writer/producers in the industry. Or that my costars—Countess Vaughn, who plays my daughter, Kim, Yvette Wilson, who plays my best friend, Andell, Dorien Wilson, who keeps me running each week as Professor Stanley Oglevee, Ken Lawson, who plays T, and Jenna Von Oy, who plays Stevie—would become like a second family. My brother has worked my career, and I've worked with some of my idols, including Isabel Sanford, aka Louise "Weezie" Jefferson from *The Jeffersons*. What a thrill it was to have this dear sweet woman on *The Parkers* as my man-hungry grandmother. I've also worked alongside the incomparable Whoopi Goldberg and Danny Glover, and shared the spotlight with a dynamic circle of sisters like Ella Joyce, Wendy Raquel Robinson, and Vanessa Bell Calloway for a benefit performance of *The Vagina Monologues*. For nearly a year, I was up at three in the morning to serve as cohost of D.C.'s top-rated WHUR morning radio show done from the comfort of bed. Steve has gotten me

My girls, Charisse and Michelle,
on an airplane trip to visit me in Los Angeles.

everything that crazy New York manager promised and more, including five figures for stand-up performances. He's kept and even exceeded his word, and the best part of it all is that we did it together—the entire family.

Today, Millicent lives with her family in Los Angeles and runs the day-to-day operations of Big City Artist Management, the talent management division Steve created, and my clothing company, Mo'Nique's Fashions. My brother Gerald is still in Baltimore, but a move is on the horizon. My parents, who've been married more than forty years, are now living a much-deserved life of luxury. The first time my mom saw the newly added apostrophe in my name, she said, What's that? I said, Baby, that's a star name. It took her a minute to understand, and she teased me whenever she saw the new moniker, but when the checks started coming in, she began to understand real quick—"Oh, that's you, baby girl!" She and my father have since moved west to share in our family's good fortune, and between her regular trips to Las Vegas, which I finance, and frequent set visits, their lives are great. In fact, it was during one of my dad's early Hollywood visits that he caught the acting bug. After seeing the hoopla, he turned to me and announced, " 'Nique, I can do this." Today, he's embarking on career number three (acting) and studying with one of the industry's leading acting coaches, Chip Fields-Hurd. For those *Good Times* fans, Miss Chip is the accomplished stage and screen actress who portrayed the evil mother of Penny (Janet Jackson's character) on the classic show. She's also the mom of actresses Kim and Alexis Fields. A few years ago Pops made his acting debut on the show, and we can't get the tape of his performance out of the VCR. After harsh Baltimore winters, fights in school, living on the road, and surviving several tumultuous relationships, I can say that life is good.

The brightest spot in my life is my handsome son, Shalon.

He's the reason why I keep going, but even he got me with a stunt he pulled a few years back. One evening, I got a call from his teacher. Shalon, she said, had been acting up in school. When he got home, I asked him why and he told me he heard voices telling him to do something bad at school that day. First, I became a Hollywood mother, took two Excedrin PM's, and drank a cocktail to figure out how this could have happened. I thought, How could my baby be crazy? I didn't want to believe it, and soon guilt got the best of me. Maybe, I reasoned, if I'd have stayed home with him instead of being on the road so much, or took him with me more, he wouldn't be talking to imaginary people, or hearing voices.

I called the teacher back and told her that I was going to keep him home for a couple of days and monitor his behavior. Every day, Shalon would get up and tell me that the voices told him that he should just relax, play outside, or take it easy. One day, they told him he was too stressed out to leave the house and should stay in bed all day. Once or twice, I even passed his room and caught him having full conversations with his imaginary friends. After about the third day, I was starting to become afraid of my own child. I didn't know what to do, so I called Stevie and asked him to come over and have a talk with him. He went into the room, stayed about five minutes, and then came out and told me, "It's bad." Shalon insisted his imaginary friend be in on the meeting with Steve.

That was it. There was no way I could live in the house with a crazy boy. It got so bad that whenever he'd walk into the room, I'd jump. Hell, I didn't know what the voices might have told him to do. The ruse finally came to an end when the television happened to be tuned to Nickelodeon. An episode of *Rugrats* was playing and Angelicka said to her mother that she didn't want to go to school because she heard voices telling her to do something bad. That's right. Shalon got me with an episode of *Rugrats*. How did I handle it, you ask? *Not* like a Hollywood mother. I handled it like a mother from Baltimore who got played. I pulled it together, then pulled a belt out of the closet and whipped his little ass. Let's just say that after that beating, school became a welcome friend.

We laugh about it now and he knows there's nothing I wouldn't do for him. As much as I love my career, if he said, "Mommy, I wish you would just stay home, I need you," I'd do it in a minute. Of course, we'd have to move out of our BIG wonderful home, leave the swimming pool behind, and the fun vacations, too. But for him, it would be worth it, because nothing is more important than family.

And I wouldn't trade mine for the world, even when they've hurt me, like Steve did with that FAT pig comment. But he's more than made up for that little slip of the tongue, and today makes sure people call me by the right name and, when they do, have got plenty of money to go along with it. As with any family, we've experienced happy times, hard times, sad times, and even times when I wanted to trade a few of them in. But I wouldn't trade anything for this journey, because it's the journey itself and the people I've met along the way that have helped shape me into the woman I am today. God has blessed us, and my goal is to bless others. If I can make people feel better about themselves and their lives, then my journey will have been fulfilled. I ask God to keep me grounded and humble and let me always say please and thank you, good morning, and good afternoon, because the minute you lose sight of what is real is the moment you've lost sight of what is important.

This is me with the hardest working manager in show business,
my brother, Steve, after he negotiated my first stage performance
in *The Vagina Monologues*

Your-Mama's-So-Fat Jokes

The next time smart-asses try to hit you with a Your-Mama's-So-Fat joke, shut 'em down with these answers:

Your mama's so FAT, after she got off the carousel, the horse limped for a week.
Mo's rebuttal: Your mama's so skinny, she can hula-hoop through a Froot Loop.

Your mama's so FAT that at the zoo the elephants started throwing her peanuts.
Mo's rebuttal: Your mama's so skinny her nipples touch.

Your mama's so FAT, her blood type is Ragu.
Mo's rebuttal: Your mama's so skinny, she looks like a mic stand.

Your mama's so FAT, instead of 501 jeans she wears 1002s.
Mo's rebuttal: Your mama's so skinny, she turned sideways and disappeared.

Your mama's so FAT, Jenny Craig did a credit check.
Mo's rebuttal: Your mama's so skinny, she inspires crackheads to diet.

Your mama's so FAT she's not on a diet she's on a triet. What y'all eating? I'll try it.
Mo's rebuttal: Your mama's so skinny, I gave her a piece of popcorn and she went into a coma.

Your mama's so FAT, she bungee-jumped and went straight to hell.

Mo's rebuttal: Your mama's so skinny, her bra fits better backward.

Your mama's so FAT, she fell in love and broke it.

Mo's rebuttal: Your mama's so skinny, she uses Chapstick as deodorant.

Your mama's so FAT, she fell in the Grand Canyon and got stuck.

Mo's rebuttal: Your mama's so skinny, if she had dreads I could grab her by the ankles and use her to mop the floors.

Your mama's so FAT, she goes in a restaurant, looks at a menu, and says okay.

Mo's rebuttal: Your mama's so skinny, she swallowed a meatball and thought she was pregnant.

Your mama's so FAT, when she backs up she beeps.

Mo's rebuttal: Your mama's so skinny, she uses a Band-Aid as a maxipad.

Your mama's so FAT, when she jumped in the ocean all the whales started singing, "We are family."

Mo's rebuttal: Your mama's so skinny, instead of calling her your parent, you call her transparent.

Your mama's so FAT, when she jumped in the air she got stuck.

Mo's rebuttal: Your mama's so skinny, you could blindfold her with dental floss.

Your mama's so FAT, the only thing keeping her from going to Jenny Craig was the door.
Mo's rebuttal: Your mama's so skinny, Jenny Craig paid her to eat.

Your mama's so FAT, she left in a pair of high heels and came back in flip-flops.
Mo's rebuttal: Your mama's so skinny, if she turned sideways and stuck out her tongue, she would look like a zipper.

Your mama's so FAT, when she put on a red T-shirt, everybody said, "Hey, Kool-Aid."
Mo's rebuttal: Your mama's so skinny, when she wore her yellow dress, she looked like a number-2 pencil.

Typical Day in the Life of a Big Girl

6:00 A.M. Wake up.

6:30 Prepare breakfast—eggs, bacon, pancakes, potatoes, fresh-squeezed OJ.

7:30 Eat breakfast.

8:00 Meditate and let the food digest.

8:30 Dress and leave for work.

8:45 Stop at Starbucks for a cup of coffee and a lemon square for the drive.

10:00 Greet everyone at the office. Grab a doughnut.

10:30 Check and return e-mails while sipping a Coke.

11:00 Check and return phone calls while snacking on chips.

11:45 Decide where to go for lunch.

1:00 P.M. Return from lunch, check voice-mail messages and new e-mails, and return calls and e-mails if necessary.

1:30 Attend afternoon business meeting, where refreshments will be served.

2:30 Midafternoon snack break.

2:45 Do a little work.

3:15 Bathroom break.

3:45 Do a little more work.

4:45 Prepare to leave work.

5:00	Leave work.
5:30	Pick up groceries for dinner.
6:00	Arrive home.
6:15	Start dinner.
7:00	Work out at the dinner table over a plate of fried chicken, collard greens, yams, macaroni and cheese, and peach cobbler.
8:00	Catch a movie on cable. Pop a bowl of popcorn to go along with it.
10:00	Prepare for bed.
11:00	"Get busy" workout session before turning in.
11:30	If the lovemaking was really good, warm up leftovers from dinner.
12:00 A.M.	Turn in for the evening.
12:10	Sleep like a baby.

Typical Day in the Life of a Skinny Girl

6:00 A.M. Get up.

6:15 Get dressed for morning jog.

6:30 Morning jog.

7:30 Return from jog. No time for breakfast, grab a granola bar. Weigh.

8:30 Arrive at the office after taking the stairs fifteen floors.

8:45 Have assistant pick up an extra-strong Starbucks coffee. Strap on ankle weights while sitting in on a conference call.

9:00 Check heart rate.

9:15 Check and return e-mails while doing leg lifts under desk.

10:00 Boss assigns a lengthy status report. Check heart rate after boss informs you it's due the next day. Another Starbucks run.

12:00 P.M. No time to go out for lunch. Have assistant pick up a salad and a third cup of Starbucks. Eat at desk.

3:00 Attend staff meeting. Get 100 leg lifts in under desk during meeting.

4:00 Back to the desk to continue work on report while exercising gluteus muscles.

5:30 While everyone is leaving for the evening, grab a fourth cup of Starbucks to prepare for late night at the office.

9:00   Leave work. Instead of the elevator, take stairs fifteen floors.

9:30   Pick up baked half skinless chicken and grilled veggies for dinner.

10:00   Jump on treadmill for an evening workout while reading *Fitness* magazine.

11:00   Finish work on report brought home from the office along with a cup of coffee to stay awake.

11:30   Watch news while completing 100 sit-ups.

12:00 A.M. Uptight from work, so no time for sex, again. Check heart rate and turn in for the evening.

12:00   Wired from coffee. Can't sleep. Pull out report and work for two more hours.

THREE

Food, Glorious Food

NEED IT, WANT IT, GOTTA HAVE IT

SOME FOLKS ENJOY A FINE WINE. Others take great pleasure in the taste of an exceptional Cuban cigar, or get a thrill from the feel of driving a fancy sports car. I happen to be a food connoisseur. That's right. French. Mexican. Italian. Soul. It really doesn't matter. I like it all. And there's nothing wrong with that, because everyone has a thing. A skinny woman's thing might be to starve to death, while mine happens to be eating. And there's nothing better than a marvelous meal followed by a delectable dessert. BIG girls, people may try to tell you something's wrong with enjoying good food, but eating is a vital part of life, especially in America. This is the richest country in the world, good food is abundant, and that's why our favorite phrase is "Supersize it." So why the hell can't the skinny seem to get the message and eat up? Trying to get a skinny bitch to pick up a fork is like trying to convince a nun to have sex—it ain't happening (can't say the same for the priests), and even if it does, the shit ain't much good, because practice makes perfect, and Lord knows this puny posse could use all the practice they can get.

And nowhere is the practice of eating and the battle of the BULGE fought more ferociously than in dining rooms across the country. It's a practice we've perfected, a happening event in the lives of BIG women. So much so that we already know what we want and the number it is on the menu. Pull up to a McDonald's drive-through, and it's, "Gimme the number one, and Supersize it." Everyone knows that's a Big Mac Combo. So why do skinny bitches act like they're seeing the menu for the first time? And, after they've studied it for ten minutes, come up with a McSalad Shaker and McSoup Combo? Who knew—or even cared—that Mickey D's made soup? The food industry has made it easy to eat on the run, so it only makes sense that we do our part and eat well. That's why food connoisseurs master the art of ordering like a science. A Quarter Pounder with cheese and a fistful of french fries, now that's some eat-while-you-drive food for your ass all day long. So is that chicken from Popeye's—just grab a chicken drumstick and go. Drumsticks are the only food with handles. When dining on the dash, you can't grip a McSalad, or slurp a McSoup. Part of being a food connoisseur is understanding which establishments give the most grub for our hard-earned dollar, the ideal days to get it, and the most important fact of all—how to obtain it at the best price—free. It's vital information like this that fuels the American economy, keeps restaurants open, and keeps business booming, but the scrawny refuse to fall in line. So, fuck 'em. Let them starve to death. In the meantime, BIG girls, we've got hamburgers, hot dogs, hors d'oeuvres, and Häagen-Dazs to handle.

After handling the stress of a hectic workweek, BIG girls need an outlet, a release, a way to let loose. You're probably thinking have some sex, and burn some calories. But I'm talking happy hours, the ideal locale to chill out, eat well, and meet men. Food connoisseurs know that finding the perfect spot requires research and observation (for example, is it a bunch of skinny folks sitting around, or a PLUMP patronage?) As the name indicates, you should be happy when you're there. The watering hole right next to your office may be geographically desirable, but if you walk in and it's nothing but peanuts and pretzels, walk out. You can't find much happiness—just more hunger—in those trifling truffles. Venture a little farther, say, to a jazz club. Jazz is usually associated with the South, and the South generally means one thing—down-home cooking. Chances are, when they put out the appetizers, it's elaborate offerings of rib tips, hot wings, egg rolls, mini-pizzas, Swedish meatballs, cheese, crackers, chips, dips, and even shrimp. And it doesn't hurt to become friends with the bartenders, or to know the cocktail waitresses on a first-name basis. If they know you, you can hit happy hour at just the right time—from beginning to end— and luck up on a fine man to buy your whiskey sours and all the free edibles you can handle. Tote a BIG enough purse, and five-o'clock munchies turn into great midnight snacks, too. And speaking of purses, the right bag makes all the difference in the world. For example, a clutch purse is usually small and narrow, only good for carrot sticks, celery, and maybe a few radishes. In other words, leave that motherfucker at home. But for maximum meals on the steal, a Louis Vuitton backpack, or shoulder bag is the perfect happy-hour accessory. Make sure it's the highest-quality handbag you can buy, and can sustain leakage like a champ. Then, you can stuff chicken wings in one area, isolate meatballs in another, and stash shrimp, still on ice, in a completely separate compartment. But you've got to know the art of getting all that food into your purse without drawing attention to yourself. Don't stand over chafing dishes and stuff it in. That's the surest way to get asked to leave. What you must do is load up your plate, then take it back to your table. Make sure everything's sectioned off—cheese on one side, chicken wings on the other, and shrimp arranged just so. That way, when you go to load it in, you won't end up with cheese in the same compartment as shrimp and egg rolls crowded next to quiche. And here's a hint for meatballs. Have your handbag slightly ajar so you can roll those babies in one at a time, or, for a true food connoisseur, all in one fell swoop. Now, if your goal is more than just a few pieces, then a supply of food storage bags is a must, too. Whether it's Hefty or Glad, zipper or snap, these durable baggies hold everything from fruits and beets to snacks and meats, or, in this case, crackers, dips, and chips— leakage and crumbs are a no-no. And lastly, don't pass up the peanuts and pretzels; they fit nicely in a zippered side compartment and just might come in handy on a long ride home.

And BIG girls, go back as many times as you'd like. After all, they put that spread out there for a reason—to get eaten. There's no reason why all that good food should go to waste. That's why knowing the help comes in handy. If they know you, they'll save you the good seats near the buffet, hook you up with extra-strong apple martinis, and stash plates of food away for you to take home. The next time you're out, observe. If there's happiness in the air, chances are there's BIG girls and food everywhere. And when we luck up on the ideal spot, unlike the skinny who keep secrets, we tell all our friends, so everyone can eat well. See how sharing and loving we are, BIG girls?

Another place where folks dine well is at an all-you-can-eat brunch. I don't know who came up with the concept of pay one price and eat as much as you can, but there's a special place in BIG heaven just for them. Those four little words are a BIG joy to us. None of that two-dishes-and-we're-done bullshit, our goal is to clean our plates, and potentially shut some shit down. In African-American households, Sunday brunch is *the* must-do event of the day, especially after a marathon Easter or Mother's Day church service. By the time the minister offers the benediction and they've teased us with that drop of grape juice and crumb of cracker for communion, we can't wait to tear out of that sanctuary and get to eatin'. And let me be very clear. We aren't doing one of those fancy-schmancy places that designates certain hours as brunch, serves a limited menu, one glass of cheap champagne and a basket of stale blueberry muffins. Hell no! We're heading to spots with full-scale productions of made-to-order omelets and waffles, carving stations of prime rib, turkey, and baked ham, chafing dishes of bacon, seafood crepes, chilled shrimp, and king crab legs. And for dessert, fuck the fruit, unless it's on a piece of cake or pie. It's chocolate-covered strawberries, pecan cheesecake, bread pudding with whiskey sauce, and apple-almond crisp—because you can't do brunch and not sample everything. Now, that's what I call comfort food.

And it's comforting to gather the entire family—BIG Mama, Mo'Dear, Lil' Mama (who's really BIG, but just short) and all the kids—and dine together at a nice restaurant. And we roll deep, too. Which means we'll need the BIGGEST table in the house because in addition to eating, brunch is also a time for bonding, fun, and fellowship—unless, of course, there's a skinny bitch in the bunch. A bony one will fuck up the flow every single time. Seeing that much food seems to send them into shock. They get fidgety and are ready to roll after nibbling on a patch of salad and a baked chicken leg. What's the rush, anyway?

Did you know that in France, dinner sometimes lasts four or five hours? The French sit down to a feast with bottles of fine wine and packs of cigarettes and just let the food flow. There's no such thing as rushing folks so they can seat another party, because rushing through a meal ruins one's digestion. They talk, eat, laugh, talk, eat, laugh, unbuckle their belts, and talk, eat, and laugh some more. I'm with that. That's how BIG girls do it, too. We pace ourselves, return for fourths, and hold contests to see who can go the distance—even if it takes all evening. For the voluptuous, eating is about relaxation. But for the thin, it's about tension. And nowhere is there more tension surrounding food than in Los Angeles.

If you know anything about Hollywood, then you know that nothing gets done in this town unless it happens over breakfast, lunch, or dinner. In fact, I'm convinced this has got to be *the* city where the phrase "Let's do lunch" originated. Folks take great pride in seeing and being seen, especially at the hottest new restaurant in town. That's why, as a food connoisseur, I thought I'd enjoy all the lunching, brunching, and munching. But damn, was I in for a rude awakening. Here, folks brunch and lunch, but its done over wheat-grass waffles and tofu tacos. I've strolled into eateries and been the BIGGEST thing in the place and opened menus that didn't have one morsel of meat on them. It was vegetable this, tofu that (what the fuck is tofu, anyway? Nobody eats that shit anywhere else but in California), and a selection of vitamins, supplements, and organic and natural foods. That's when I realized how folks stayed so damn thin in this town—it's all the alfalfa sprouts, miracle tonics, and Zone diets. For a moment I thought I was in a zone—the damn Twilight Zone.

This city is full of human sticks that look as if they haven't had a bite since birth. Some of these starved starlets are so frail they make me want to shove a Twinkie into their mouths and scream, "Eat, feeble heifer, eat."

But it would take more than a box of Twinkies to fix what's wrong in this town. With so many top-rated restaurants and deals getting done over food, you'd think there'd be a better, meatier selection. Instead, it's like the land before time where zombies wander around and pass out because all they eat is juice, fruit, and carrot sticks. For BIG folks, Hollywood can be a headache—a hunger headache.

And that's what I got when a business associate invited me to dine at one of Beverly Hills's swankiest and most extravagant restaurants. The establishment was owned by a top chef who spent years perfecting a fusion of food to please the palates of picky people in Tinseltown. Finally, his particular blend had become the toast of the industry, the latest BIG thing, and had drawn magazine food critics, television cooking shows, and customers to his chic eatery to sample the nouvelle cuisine. Everyone in the city—including me—who bought into the hype was trying to get a table. After weeks of failed attempts, a business associate pulled a few strings and got us in to discuss a potential film project.

The moment I stepped in the door, I realized there wasn't a F.A.T. honey in sight. That should have been my first clue that shit was about to get funky. This is Beverly Hills, land of Botox (injections of a toxin that makes frown lines go away) and fake boobs. So, I didn't think twice about this typical Hollywood hot spot. It was the usual—a crowded bar, high-powered movers and shakers conducting business on cell phones, and skinny pinups on the stroll. Even the servers looked as if they stepped right off a silver screen. From the looks of things, there wasn't much eating—just lots of schmoozing—going on.

It was the first time I'd be meeting my dinner date, a well-known talent agent. When she finally arrived (that's another Hollywoodism—nobody's ever on time), I did a guesstimate and determined that she was about a size six. Girlfriend seemed polite and before dinner talked briefly about her move from the Midwest and her early ambitions as an actress. I couldn't quite determine whether she was a cool thin six, or a skinny evil one, so, I made a mental note: *If this bitch gets crazy, she's gonna get it.* I didn't want size to influence my opinion, especially since she was picking up the tab. It seems her success came not as an A-list actor but as a high-powered talent agent behind some of the industry's most successful leading ladies. This prompted another note: *Sitting before me is a frustrated bitch who never achieved plan A, so she's settled for plan B.* This woman rambled on for a few more minutes, and eventually the conversation shifted to more personal issues about her single status, and how she transformed her life. It turned out that she was once a size eighteen, but after years of hating her looks, she decided to seek medical help. Mental note: *L.A.'s warped beauty standards have caused this neurotic heifer to crack under pressure.* A top doctor who'd worked miracles on countless Hollywood hotties immediately changed her eating habits, referred her to one of the most popular personal trainers in town, and encouraged her to meditate. It all sounded like a bunch of New Age metaphysical, spiritual-enlightenment mumbo jumbo, but I acted interested, though I wasn't clear why she was pouring her life story out to me. After twenty minutes I began to do some meditating of my own—about how good the food was going to taste—as this sermon dragged on for ten more minutes. She championed the virtues of vegetarianism and swore it changed her life. I was beginning to dislike where this little talk was headed. Eventually this woman revealed her true colors with one simple statement: "Have you ever considered losing weight, Mo'Nique? Vegetarianism will change your life." Why do skinny bitches always want to convert the F.A.T.? What makes them think we aren't happy, healthy, vibrant, and sexy, just the way we are? I had to hand it to girlfriend, she was smooth with her shit, but I've never taken humiliation about my weight without a fight, and I wasn't about to start now, especially coming from a woman who used to be one of us. You'd think she could look past weight and understand that we don't have to all be a size six to make it in this tiny-ass town. Clearly, she had crossed over the enemy lines and lost more than weight— this bitch lost her damn mind. I about lost mine, too. That's when I looked her blankly in the face and replied, "I like chicken, ribs, and steak too much to give them up. And I've got a man at home who loves ALL of this. Who's at home waiting on you?" Call me evil, but at the time I was hungrier than a hostage, and the mere thought of eating nuts, grains, and twigs made me snap. There are three things you better not fuck with—my precious son, my man, and my food. I don't think I sent this woman a help-me-lose-weight vibe. I guess she assumed that as a tantalizing twenty-two, I must be miserable like her. After my brief tirade, sistergirl got the message, chuckled uncomfortably, and took a sip of her lemon water. Then she picked up her menu, along with her face, from the floor and tried to switch gears. I picked my menu up, too, because just thinking about her audacity only made me hungrier. Mental note: *Score one for BIG girls.*

That may have been the end of our FAT chat, but it was only the beginning of this dining disaster. As I studied the menu, there didn't seem to be one item that sounded very appetizing. So imagine how my dread turned to delight when the waiter announced a filet mignon platter as the special of the evening. I added a Caesar salad to that filet mignon and was ready to chow down. But my dinner date, on the other hand, was ready for a game of twenty questions—and proceeded to ask about every damn thing on the menu. Is the lettuce organic? Is the cheese tempeh (what the fuck is tempeh?)? Does the salad dressing contain dairy? And could she please have organic butter? I swear this crazy bitch, and the skinny waiter serving us, sounded as if they were speaking a foreign language that I didn't understand—or care to. All I wanted to do was dive into that salad. To deal with this crazy woman, I was going to need food—fast. My mouth was ready, too. So, in anticipation of what was too come, I buttered a piece of cracked whole wheat bread and waited with bated breath. But, baby, when that little-ass salad hit the table, it was three leaves of lettuce and one cherry tomato—I kid you not. That shit didn't do anything but piss me the hell off. That is, until the steak arrived. Now, in Baltimore, where I come from, if you order a steak, the shit is usually served on a BIG plate with meat hanging off the sides, and a PLUMP baked potato, swimming in butter, sour cream, and bacon bits—but not in LALA Land. My first thought was, Where's the beef? Because nothing on that plate even remotely resembled meat. The waiter pointed it out, and eventually I found that morsel of meat cowering under a garden of carrots, broccoli, and cauliflower. That shit was so damn leathery, I didn't know whether to eat it or put it on my foot and wear it. I glanced across the table at my dinner date, who was eyeing her chopped vegetable salad with tofu croutons and alfalfa sprout dressing (served on the side, of course) like it was a Thanksgiving feast.

Then she leaned in and whispered, "Doesn't this look great?" I told the waiter there must be some mistake—I didn't order the vegetable plate. He assured me it was indeed the petite filet mignon platter, then snickered as he walked away. Right then, it clicked. This bitch had tricked me. This was an expensive health food restaurant and that steak wasn't really steak. With dread, I choked down this healthy meal and noticed that my dinner date was also struggling to finish hers. After two bites, she told the waiter to take it away. She was stuffed, and I was still starving.

And starved wasn't the way I wanted to conduct a business meeting. So I proceeded to fill up on more bread and butter, but the soy butter wasn't doing it for me either, and my hunger headache was getting worse. It was going to be hell to focus on a semi-empty, fully upset stomach. In fact, girlfriend could have pitched a blockbuster starring Denzel Washington and me, stranded butt-naked on a beach, and it wouldn't have mattered. My thoughts were on another scene; one that starred me and a double cheeseburger. So I did the polite thing, excused myself, and headed to the rest room. Though a bit shaky, I found my way to the back door and escaped from that overpriced hellhole like a runaway slave bound for the promised land. My first stop was Fatburger, where I tore into a double Fatburger with cheese. Miraculously, after just one bite, the shakes subsided, and my headache was a thing of the past.

Dining out should be an enjoyable experience. But that's not going to happen as long as the skinny—as hungry as they are—refuse to eat and ridicule us for wanting to enjoy our fair share. It will also remain a challenge until restaurants cater to a clientele that really matters—folks who like to chow down. Instead, they insult BIG eaters by squeezing in too many

tables, prohibiting those of us who require roomier accommodations from comfortably getting our grub on. And please,
hire a staff based on food knowledge rather than good looks.
Like the time a couple of friends and I went to a steak house
and asked the waitress, a cutesy little white girl who weighed
about ninety pounds and whose ribs were poking through her
size-two uniform, which she recommended, the rib eye or the
porterhouse steak. Her response: "I don't eat meat, but the rib
eye is a popular choice." That's the stupidest shit I've ever
heard. Lie to me. Tell me the T-bone can't be beat, but whatever you do, don't tell me, standing in a steak house, that you
don't eat meat. Because a vegetarian working in a steak house
makes about as much damn sense as a one-legged man in an
ass-kicking contest. There should be a law that to seek
employment at Black Angus, you must eat meat, and be com-
petent enough to answer simple food-related questions. Is
that too damn much to ask?

And here's a question I'd like to ask restaurant owners and
managers. Who exactly is your clientele—the HEFTY and
hungry, or the fickle and finicky? Here's a hint: BIG eaters will
keep your doors open and keep you employed. That's why you
should greet us with a smile when you see us coming and seat
us up front so you can get some free advertisement of how
good the food is. I'm telling you, skinny folks will turn on you
in a minute. On Saturday they're into sushi. Sunday, it's vegetarian, and by Monday, chicken and fish only. And when they
open menus, they're eyeing the left side—the appetizers. In
fact, their favorite words—starter, snack, cup, small plate, first
course, mini, and petite—are the ones we try to avoid. I don't
want anything petite, especially a juicy piece of meat. When
healthy eaters dine out, our words of choice are platter, feast,
hearty, generous, and of course my all-time favorite, all-you-

can-eat. Those are adjectives that tell BIG eaters we'll be FULL.

But even all-you-can-eat can be deceiving if left in the hands of skinny folks. Several years ago, a certain seafood restaurant that has a lobster as its logo advertised "all-you-can-eat-shrimp" and a friend of mine, a BIG brother who loved seafood, decided to drop by to get his shrimp fix on. At first, things were cool. The perky little waitress was polite, and prompt at replenishing the plates he happily consumed. But three hours after his arrival, things went horribly awry. He noticed a change in behavior. Suddenly the waiters were whispering, pointing, and avoiding his table. The cooks were coming out of the kitchen to check him out, and management was glaring at him, too. When he attempted to request more platters of shrimp, a manager approached the table instead, tapped him on the shoulder, and announced, "I'm sorry, sir, but you've eaten our entire supply." Never mind that he'd been there since noon, had seen a shift change, and polished off twenty plates.

The point is, if management had done its job properly and ordered enough damn seafood, then they wouldn't have had to go around to each table and announce that the BIG gentleman by the window ate up everything. My poor friend had to endure stares from the entire restaurant. But that wasn't the end of it. Management then proceeded to covertly give everyone a coupon for a return visit. When he inquired about a coupon, a skinny manager handed one over with a stipulation—to call ahead next time. Okay, now what's wrong with this picture? I'll tell you. First, don't advertise all-you-can-eat and not have enough for customers to eat. Second, what's up with the call-ahead-next-time bullshit? That's harassment. Clearly, this was a management problem, or should I say, a mismanagement problem. The fine gentleman strolled in and ordered what was advertised, and was humiliated in the process. That's the kind of shit Mo'Nique is here to stop— BIG abuse. Restaurants had better plan accordingly, because BIG eaters are coming and we want enough food and LARGE enough tables—shit, make 'em banquet size if you have to—to sit comfortably.

And speaking of accommodating us, ease up on all the unnecessary shit you put on tables, too. When you're BIG, space is a must, and more space allows for additional food in its place. So stop with all the silverware—three knives and forks—you put on tables. It's pointless, and it confuses folks. A dinner fork picks up a leaf of lettuce or a pat of butter and slices into a delicious piece of cheesecake just as well as a but-ter knife or dessert spoon. If we want extra utensils, we'll request them.

We'll also request condiments to make a meal tastier. Because there's nothing more frustrating than getting your mouth all tuned up for a good lunch only to be told, "Sorry, ma'am, we don't carry that." That's some upsetting shit. Chicken is chicken, but hot sauce turns chicken from ordinary to extraordinary. So make sure you've got it. It's a must-do. So is real sugar, because trying to get a BIG GULP–size glass of tea sweet with those little blue and pink packets of Equal or Sweet'N Low is next to impossible. Nowadays, so is ordering a meal that's flavorful. This is another problem created by the skinny. Restaurants are so afraid to spice shit up that they put everything on the side, forgetting that the key to a flavorful meal is to simmer all the ingredients together. But if you should happen upon a bland meal, don't let that stop you, just roll with your own stash—real sugar, Lawry's Seasoned Salt, and Crystal Louisiana hot sauce travel with me everywhere, and I won't hesitate to whip them out to spice some shit up. These are all areas of improvement that should be a foremost concern for restaurants.

One of my primary concerns is tolerance—and metabolism. For years, I've tried to drive the point home that BIG folks require LARGER portions. You may get full from a two-piece chicken dinner, for me it takes six pieces. You may eat dessert after a meal, while I like to have mine on the plate along with everything else. But that's a foreign idea to the skinny, thus making it nearly impossible for us to peacefully coexist when dining together. That's why, after years of humiliation, I refuse to dine with them. They aren't interested in understanding our dietary needs. Instead, skinny folks shake their heads in disgust and stare when the six-piece cat-fish dinner with hush puppies arrives, and scrutinize every spoonful of peach cobbler. What if BIG girls ridiculed their idiotic choices, like a cup of soup or half a sandwich? Or rolled our eyes at all that damn calorie and carbohydrate counting? Shit, you need a master's degree in carbology to understand how that shit works. Skinny folks carry handbooks and diagrams to make sure they can eat certain foods. Once, four skinny bitches at a table next to me ordered one salad and split it four ways. Another time, a bony one pulled out a scale and weighed a chicken breast right at the table, then checked her watch to make sure it wasn't past her six o'clock food cutoff time.

And what's the rush, anyway? Some of the best meals occur after midnight. That's why I love Las Vegas, the land of the midnight buffet. BIG folks can hit the jackpot, then hit the buffet and eat well with their winnings, especially at the five-dollar buffets. Shit, you could be poor and hungry at noon, hit the jackpot, and for five dollars spend the evening enjoying an endless selection. In fact, at buffets, we encourage our friends to enjoy extra helpings of chicken marsala, ask if they'd like to sample our smothered pork chops, and persuade them to go back for fifths—and bring us back a few more slices of roast beef while they're up. And it doesn't just stop with dinner. Dessert is a must-do, too. While skinny women skip the sweets so they can watch their figures, BIG girls do dinner, then try to figure out which dessert to do first. After all, you need something sweet after a good meal, or it doesn't seem satisfying. Kind of like a cigarette after sex. Next time you're out, take a look around. For the table of BIG folks, there's laughter in the air and plates piled high everywhere. Then check out the skinny table. No laughter—just carb counting, food weighing, and watch checking to make sure it's daylight. I swear, skinny folks take the joy out of dining out.

That's probably why they also bypass food courts in malls. Now, I like to shop like the next glamour puss, but that shop-till-you-drop bullshit is ridiculous, especially when you consider the wonderful food courts in malls these days; Cuisine from all over the world, a food connoisseur's dream. Damn it, if we're going to spend twenty hours shopping, eating is a must—at least twice, maybe three times. Let's browse the food court, check out all the new eateries, and sample free grub on toothpicks. Now, that's my idea of a productive shopping day.

All jokes aside, I've observed some of my BIG sisters at food courts and in buffet lines, even stood behind a few of you, and it's a little scary. Slow down. Pace yourselves. The food ain't going anywhere. And speaking of not going anywhere, it wouldn't hurt some of you to take a walk every once in a while. Stretch your legs. Move around. Don't keep sending your girl back to get you more plates—get them your damn self. And some of y'all pile them so high it resembles the

Leaning Tower of Pisa. A word of advice: each time you go back for more, get regular-size portions. Because the last thing you want is for a BIG, heavy plate of prime rib to snap your wrist, putting you out of commission for a while—that really would be a tragedy.

Tragic is also the word I'd use to describe the state of grocery stores these days. Is it my imagination, or do potato chip bags have more air than chips, is a loaf of bread barely six slices, and does a value pack of chicken wings look more like a single serving? Get to the register, and the cashier wants a hundred dollars for two bags of food. It's a rip-off. That's why I'm a fan of warehouse stores like Costco and Sam's Club. If you've never been to one of these GIANT supermarkets, do yourself a favor and get a membership. They definitely had FAT folks in mind when they thought up that idea—and the store layout. Nice, wide aisles, and everything from fine jewelry and stereos to fresh USDA choice beef, Grade A chicken, fresh seafood, prepared meals, deli platters, rotisserie chicken, ribs, and frozen entrees, all in one location—a BIG girl's dream.

And speaking of dreams, let me switch gears for a moment. BIG girls, I know you have dreams. Hell, we all do. Mine was to become a star, and nothing would stop me from fulfilling my destiny. I want that to be your attitude, too. Find your passion, and like Nike says, "Just Do It." If you do hair, become the best damn hairdresser at the salon. Then open up a chain of your own. If your cooking makes folks want to slap someone silly, create a catering company and feed the masses, and if the good Lord blessed you with an awesome set of pipes (like my girls Jennifer Holiday, Aretha Franklin, and Miss Patti LaBelle) then, baby, you better sing your heart out. Your mission isn't to prove that you're worthy. It's to be happy and focused on the beautiful gifts the Creator blessed you with. Never let anyone—especially a skinny, confused bitch—take you off your game. Perhaps one day these twisted sisters will learn to accept us—regardless of our exterior—and the unique beauty we possess. But you can't get your blessings if you aren't healthy.

Which brings me to another important point. Sure, I encourage BIG girls to eat what pleases them, but please, be sensible about it, too. Listen to well-intentioned advice from loved ones when they tell you that your wheezing and labored breaths are worrisome, or that your unhealthy eating habits may be causing your body to break. Eat to live, don't just live to eat. Pay attention to your body, because nothing is more important than your health. I know it's hard, but some of you must begin to enjoy your favorite foods in moderation. Go slow. Pace yourself. Cut calories when and wherever possible.

A good place to start is with that Dr. Pepper you love so much. Next time, order a diet Dr. Pepper to go along with your three-piece chicken and biscuit dinner, instead. That's twenty-five calories gone right off the top. See how easy that is? And BIG girls, I know you're going to curse me for this, but three desserts at one time is far too much for anyone. You know what ice cream tastes like. And no, you don't have to eat the entire pint of Chunky Monkey ice cream in one sitting. Save some for later. Just say no. Push away from the table. Have a little willpower. Unless, of course, it's one of BIG Mama's homemade Sock-It-to-Me cakes—then dive on in, girlfriend, because special occasions are exempt, and you can always start cutting back tomorrow.

Of course, you know that none of this would be a problem if it weren't for a certain segment of the population. The real culprits in all of this are skinny bitches. If you're like me, you can't stand to see good food go to waste. If the skinny would just play fair—and eat their share—we wouldn't have to.

MO'S RESTAURANT GUIDE TO GOOD FOOD AND PLENTY OF IT

NATIONAL CHAINS

POPEYE'S CHICKEN Wings are bigger. Selection is greater. Desserts are tastier. And, the red beans and rice will make you wanna slap your mama.

RED LOBSTER The all-you-can-eat specialties are the highlight of this seafood haunt.

CHEESECAKE FACTORY The selection of cheesecake alone is enough of a reason to go, but in addition to that, the menu is like a mini catalog. BIG girls won't be disappointed. There might even be enough left to tote home in a doggie bag.

THE OLIVE GARDEN It's the next best thing to being in Italy. The never-ending pasta, salad, and soup is a BIG girl's best friend.

HOMETOWN BUFFET Mexican. Italian. Chinese. American. There's a lot of everything at these, cafeteria style, restaurants.

SIZZLER Steak. Salad. Seafood. And plenty of it!

PONDEROSA STEAKHOUSES/BONANZA STEAKHOUSES Giddy up, cowboy. Home on the range was never quite like the spread you'll find here.

KRISPY KREME All I've gotta say is, when that Hot Donuts Now sign lights up, you'll damn near have an accident trying to get into this mouth-watering doughnut shop.

MO'NIQUE'S FAVORITE RESTAURANTS, LISTED BY CITY

BEAUTIFUL RESTAURANT
397 Auburn Avenue, NW
Atlanta, GA
(404) 223-0080

GLADYS KNIGHT & RON WINANS CHICKEN & WAFFLES
529 Peachtree Street, NE
Atlanta, GA
(404) 874-9393

SOUTHERN BLUES SOUL FOOD
3613 Offutt Road
Randallstown, MD
(410) 521-1830

LAKE TROUT
5401 Reisterstown Road
Baltimore, MD
(410) 764-7240

MICAH'S CAFETERIA
6841 Loch Raven Blvd.
Towson, MD
(410) 321-1811

STEVIE'S CREOLE CAFÉ
16911 Ventura Blvd.
Encino, CA
(818) 528-3500

HAROLD & BELLE'S
2920 West Jefferson
Los Angeles, CA
(323) 735-9023

ROSCOE'S HOUSE OF CHICKEN & WAFFLES
1514 N. Gower Street
Los Angeles, CA
(323) 466-7453

MARY'S PIT BBQ
1106 Jefferson Street
Nashville, TN
(615) 256-7696

HAROLD'S CHICKEN SHACK
636 S. Wabash Avenue
Chicago, IL
(312) 362-0442
or
7310 S. Halsted Street
Chicago, IL
(773) 723-9006

B. SMITH RESTAURANT
50 Massachusetts Avenue, NE
Washington, DC
(202) 289-6188

JIMMY'S UPTOWN
2207 Adam Clayton Powell Blvd.
New York, NY
(212) 491-4000

F.A.T. Girls' Survival Tips

DINING—

* You pick the restaurant.

* Travel with a personal stash that should include: real sugar, Crystal Louisiana hot sauce, and Lawry's Seasoned Salt.

* If it's a chic restaurant and food is scarce, order double.

FOUR

Sexy Is More than a Size

SHOPPING HORROR STORIES OF A FULL-FIGURED FASHIONATA

I REFUSE TO WEAR FAT fashions. Muumuus definitely won't do. Because, BIG girls, we can't shine all covered up in coat-dresses, turtleneck sweaters, and muumuus. And speaking of them, who came up with that damn name, anyway? Probably a skinny bitch trying to be clever. Well, the shit ain't clever or cute, it's offensive. I don't care if you do try to dress it up and respell it M-U-U-M-U-U, it still sounds like the noise a cow makes, and let me clear some shit up before we go any further: BIG GIRLS ARE NOT COWS, WE ARE ATTRACTIVE, VIVACIOUS SEX KITTENS. Some of us are even lionesses. And our loveliness shouldn't be concealed. It must be revealed—to the world. That's why, if it's cute, classy, and in my size, it's going in my closet. Because I want, need, have to have pretty clothing that flatters my lovely legs, captivat-

ing cleavage, and dazzling derriere. Those are just three of
my best assets. I've got a question, BIG girls. Do you know
your best feature, the thing that makes you fabulous? If not,
then baby, I want you to put this book down right now and
remove all your clothes. Then step in front of a mirror—a
full-length mirror—and take all of your loveliness in. You
may be tempted to run, but just stand there for a moment and
study every line, every curve and every damn dimple. Some of
you may have to meet your legs again, since it's been a while
since you two have seen each other. Hey, I ain't hatin'. I'm
just keepin' it real. Study your physique. Then pick a part—
or two—that pleases you and say those three words every
woman should say at least twice a day: "Damn, I'm fine."
That's right. Say it loud, "I'm F.A.T and I'm proud." SIZ-
ABLE sisters, make that your mantra, because if you've got
the goods like me, then muumuus need to be removed from
your closet.

So do the labels of skinny white men named Calvin and
Tommy, who don't have a clue about real women, or how to
dress us. Who made these guys fashion authorities, anyway?
In case you hadn't noticed, Calvin Klein is more partial to
skeletons. So unless you blow in the wind when you walk,
don't even think about CK. He should rearrange those two
letters. Because expensive Kid Clothes is really what he
designs. And, y'all, we really shouldn't be surprised, because
Cal's been up to his antics for decades. In the eighties, his
muse, Brooke Shields, preached that nothing should come
between you and your Calvins. Nothing, that is, but a yeast
infection. Then, he ushered in the sisterhood of the waif with
Kate Moss as his poster child for the malnourished. Calvin's
real obsession seems to be getting the starved into his suits.
Since when does looking good and dressing well mean having

Me in the Bahamas as part of the WHUR morning radio team.
(L–R) TC, me, musician Musiq, and John Monds.

to starve to death? Busy women don't have time to munch on lettuce cups all day or work out for hours.

Looking good is about more than a name on a label—it's about how we look and feel in it. But it's hard to look good in a Tommy tag if you're BIG-boned. Even though the Hilfiger Corporation claims that it's dedicated to living the spirit of the American Dream and asserts that by respecting one another we can reach all cultures and communities, just once, it would be nice if Tommy reached into the FLUFFY community when casting his ads. Instead, Tommy models look like Q-Tips with hair. The only thing I can say to TH is, maybe one day "he'll figure" out a way to get BIG girls into his britches. And when he does, I'll be the first one to shout "Heeey" to him. But before I write those two—and other wayward designers—off completely, let me school them to a fashion fact.

Today, the average American woman is not a size two, or even a size eight. She's a fabulous fourteen—a double-digit sister with hips, belly, and thighs. And whether designers want to acknowledge it or not, she's the new shape of fashion. Some of us have BIG butts and nothing up front, others have been blessed with a beautiful bosom, and that's about it. While there are a few who've had entire songs written about them. That's right, they're called brickhouses. And contrary to popular belief, we brickhouses are conscious consumers who buy what we like, travel where we want, and earn the disposable income to select brands that make us feel like valued consumers. And it's a shame that in 2003, with our $32 billion buying power, we still can't find fashionable clothing that can be purchased off-the-rack—instead of through a catalog. Listen up! FULL-BODIED sisters ain't going anywhere, and we damn sure ain't dying to get skinny, so deal with us.

But for them to deal with us is probably about as hard as it is for us to deal with some of today's crazy trends. Trust me, the average American woman isn't interested in sporting baby tees and low-rise jeans. There ain't enough material there. What she would like are barely-there black cocktail dresses, rhinestone-studded jeans, and fun, flirty fashions that showcase her curves in fabrics that aren't flimsy or that don't fall apart after just one wash. Good luck, BIG girls, because chances are those fashions don't exist. Or, if they do, they're stashed upstairs next to the sheets, or down in the basement. I swear, if forced to take another escalator to the top floor of a department store, or told to schlep over to a separate building just to find my size (yes, Salon Z at Saks Fifth Avenue in Beverly Hills, I'm talking to you), I may stage a F.A.T.-girl picket line. BIG girls, you know the drill. You hit the mall with a cool thin one, and what do you see? Gorgeous fashions beautifully displayed throughout the main floor in colors to die for. Something catches your eye, you get excited and search in vain to find your size, but the LARGEST they make is an eight. For a moment you ponder squeezing your size-eighteen ass into that eight, hoping it will miraculously fit, but reconsider when you recall how they had to cut you out of a skin-tight dress on your last shopping spree. After going through three racks of cute clothing and coming up empty, you glance over at your girl. She's got a handful of cute shit, and you've got nothing—but an attitude. When you ask the salesgirl for a size eighteen, her skinny ass (because there's never a BIG salesgirl on the main floor) tells you those sizes can be found in "Macy Woman" and points you toward the escalator. (By the way, why do Macy's—and countless other retailers—call their departments for the FULL-FIGURED "Woman"? Perhaps it's because even they know real women

I was a guest at the Just Between Sisters Retreat in the Bahamas.
This is me with New York news anchor Brenda Blackmon.

have curves). As much as you hate it, you and your girl are forced to part, go your separate ways, never to cross paths again—until it's time to go. You wave good-bye, journey to the back of the store, and mount the up escalator. The moment you step onto the floor, you're assaulted by dull, matronly tent dresses that could sleep a family of four under them in ugly prints and jail stripes, and polyester pants in brown and black. There's nothing in Macy Woman that even remotely resembles the cute gear displayed on the main floor. Why? Because we're the forgotten women, the ones designers don't believe deserve fine clothing. Frustration sets in, and you become so fed up that all you can do is head to the food court and drown your sorrows in a hot dog with mustard, catsup, and extra relish, a Cinnabon, and a Diet Coke. After a horrible shopping day, you meet back up with your girl. She's got twenty shopping bags filled with fly shit and all you've got is a doggie bag from lunch.

That's why it's time for a new trend for P.H.A.T. women tired of paying for expensive duds that don't fit right. When will retailers realize that we want awesome accessories, sensational scarves, plunging necklines, and suits that hit our hips just right, too? Instead, they insult us by assuming we're more interested in shopping for sheets and George Foreman grills (though George's little gadget is a knockout in the kitchen, and for some of you, also by the bed) than cute clothes. Though stores *should* offer us sexy stuff, instead they perpetuate divide-and-conquer tactics, separating the BIG and small with skinny fashions displayed beautifully throughout the store and a limited selection of PLUS sizes shoved against the wall, upstairs, in the back.

And if you think upstairs, or the back of a department store, is where FULL-FIGURED fashionatas should shop,

This is one of my *Parkers* publicity shots.
Baby, you couldn't tell me I wasn't a star when I took this one.

think again. You have no idea how tiring it is to trudge all the way to the escalator, then have to walk to the back of the store just to locate our section. They may think we don't know what's up, but I'm on to the evil schemes of the profit-hungry fashion industry and here's a warning: make size twos that look like twenty-twos and put them side by side, or watch your profits plummet. BIG girls want what the size six is wearing, except in our size, and we aren't going to continue to sit back and be insulted, and then hand over our hard-earned dollars for some damn tent dresses. And please, stop with the one-size-fits-all label. Too many F.A.T. girls, starved for chic clothes, are at home right now trying to squeeze into a "one-size-fits-all" dress. I want to know which "all" they're talking about, because when we put on a one-size-fits-all, all it fits is about one damn thigh. The one-size-fits-all label is more than a lie. It's life-threatening. A BIG girl could pop a kidney trying to get into one of those contraptions. Manufacturers still don't get that they can't just cut a straight size garment larger and call it plus size. They've got to study the various shapes of women and take into consideration whether the garment will be flattering on us.

It would also be nice if fashion editors took into consideration their audience. Where are all the FULL-FIGURED fashionatas? They don't exist on the pages of *Vogue* and *Cosmopolitan*. Pick up one of these style bibles, and you're liable to see a mirage of meager models airbrushed and digitally altered beyond size, shape, and in some cases, even skin tone. BIG girls don't believe the hype—folks are fatter than they appear. Until fashion editors PLUMP up, the woman-as-toothpick syndrome will continue to prevail, but we can't place the blame squarely on the shoulders of designers and high-fashion glossies. Even publications that claim to pro-

mote the HEAVY are guilty of trickery. If you don't believe
me, consider this. Most plus-size lines begin at a size fourteen, and if you take a good look, that's usually who's showcased on magazine pages. It's as if size thirty-two sisters don't
exist, or don't deserve to see themselves in magazine spreads
and on fashion runways. And speaking of runways, the only
way we're gonna see ourselves represented on a catwalk is if
we knock over—and step on—a few terrible twos, because at
the end of the runway, that's who's strutting her stuff in our
clothes.

There are a couple of major retailers that specialize in—
and make a fortune off—FAT folks, but guess how they
reward us for our loyal patronage? By getting the enemy to
model their wares, of course. That's right. A few years ago,
one of the country's largest retailers of plus-size fashions was
in search of new models. A friend, a talented and beautiful
twenty, was thrilled when the company called with an offer to
become a fit model (fit models are the the ideal body type
designers select to create samples). While she was ecstatic for
the opportunity, her real dream was to become a high-paid
print and runway mannequin. After months of unsuccessful
attempts, girlfriend was disappointed when a company representative told her she wasn't the right type. She later found
out that the right type was her nemesis, an evil eight. Okay, I
don't know about you, but that's the craziest shit I've ever
heard. A full-figured woman isn't the right type to model
FULL-FIGURED clothing, but a size eight is? See, that's the
kind of idiotic shit that happens when sticks stick together—
they take over and hire their bony buddies. My stunning,
statuesque friend couldn't get a shot because an evil eight was
getting padded up to take her place—and her dream. It's these
dirty little secrets and money-hungry evil ones that make it

This photo was taken at the Edmondson High School Ring dance. I was
fourteen years old and my date was Kevin Pride.

tough for BIG girls to get ahead, and one of the reasons some of us go home and eat.

And I really don't mean to criticize fashion outlets—most offer chic, stylish, and even sexy gear—but damn if they don't insult us before we even step foot in the place. Malnourished mannequins in a window don't exactly put me in a mood to shop, and neither does a scrawny saleswoman trying to make a commission. If these specialty stores really wanted to get HEFTY honeys in the mood to spend, then they'd place dolls on display that have a few extra pounds and rolls on them, and set up a smoothie stand in the corner of the store. Shit, a nice refreshing drink might move us to drop a few hundred dollars, but only if we'll be handing it to someone with FAT fingers who respects our sizable girth. For the CHUNKY but funky, it's still a subliminal message that skinny is in, and F.A.T.— fuck that. Skinny ain't all that, and shopping with the tiny can be treacherous business, especially at the mall, which is where my CURVY crusade commenced.

As a teen, hanging out at the mall and dressing well played key roles in my life. So at fifteen I took a job at Hutzler's, a high-end retailer in Baltimore. Like most department stores, Hutzler's didn't give a damn about plus-size fashions, or where they placed them. Walk into the store, and it was neat and orderly on the main floor. Then take a ride upstairs, and it was what-the-hell-happened-up-here? Skinny-ass mannequins were pinned with ugly clothes so that it would look like they fit, clothes were thrown about on tables, and the tore-up dressing rooms had their doors hanging off the hinges. As Hutzler's new full-figured salesgirl, something had to be done, and Mo'Nique was gonna do it. After I disrupted a few sales meetings, stuffed the suggestion box with BIG ideas, and tried to convince management to change the layout of the store,

This is my good friend, Ronda Bell, owner of Ronda's Boutique. She hired me to be a full-figure model and we're still friends to this day.

folks knew Mo meant business, which spelled trouble for my immediate supervisor, a hard-nosed woman named Miss Doris. Y'all, once I make my mind up, I can be a handful. So, management instructed Miss Doris to keep an eye on me. But I wasn't worried about her evil ass, because as the self-appointed advocate for the AMPLE, my job was to take on the establishment, stand up for the underdog. Shit, hook BIG girls up. And I took my assignment very seriously. But Miss Doris wasn't interested in hearing the rants of a FULL-FIGURED teen, or about to take seriously my veiled threats to redesign the store. She also underestimated the lengths my rebellious spirit would go to, to fight FAT injustice. This old woman was cranky, out of touch, and coming up on retirement. So she just repeated the same tired line every day: "Mo'Nique, you can't change Hutzler's. That's just the way it is." The way it was got so bad that the only way for Miss D to keep her eye on me was to assign me to dressing-room duty—and she did it every chance she got. But I wasn't about to be cooped up in a fitting room, or allow this woman and her cronies to intimidate me. So every evening during my five-o'clock-until-closing shift, I'd slip away and move a few choice pieces down to the main floor. This covert operation went on for nearly six months until management caught on to the ruse and moved everything back to its original place. Though the BIG clothes never stayed on the main floor very long, for the few days that I did walk in and observe my hand-iwork, it felt damn good. By the time management issued its final warning, I was already on to a new thrill—the employee discount.

Since Hutzler's wanted to play hardball—by refusing to give BIG clothes the same respect—I decided to stick it to them in other ways. The employee discount seemed to be the perfect place to start. And though I'm ashamed to admit it now, as a CHUBBY teen, working part-time, and paying to look good was impossible—and I wasn't about to dip into my lunch money. So I helped myself to a few choice pieces, took them home, and it was a nip here, a tuck there, and voilà, new, more revealing outfits were born. One of my favorites was a pale green sweater that I removed the sleeves from, tied around my waist, and sported with a little black miniskirt to school. By senior year, high school had become my runway, and the students my lunchtime audience. And, baby, folks anticipated a Mo fashion show, it was always unusual, outlandish, and—courtesy of Hutzler's. And Hutzler's remained my main source until Ronda's Boutique came to town and offered an even better deal—a new weekly outfit to accompany my paycheck.

Soon, my fashion flair grew right along with everything else. By the time I landed a job as a customer service representative at MCI in Atlanta, I was clean as the Board of Health, daily. So I didn't think anything of it when a size two stopped in the hallway and complimented me on a pair of alligator sling-back pumps. She wasn't a bad-looking girl, just thin, which always makes me a bit leery. This girl was new to the company and to town, but I couldn't figure out if this was a cool one or a skinny evil one in disguise, especially since the evil ones tend to start out cool, then flip the script and trip. This girl seemed friendly, so I invited her to join a group of us for weekly happy hour. Girlfriend happily accepted. She was fun, easygoing, and most important, kept up with us at the buffet. Before long, we were fast friends and hung together every weekend.

Once we had plans for an evening on the town, and that meant hitting the mall. Now, I'm all for folks looking good, and often these things take time, but this damn girl was ridiculous. She arrived at the house before breakfast, ready to

Even in high school, the hair was laid. This is my
high school graduation photo from Milford Mill High School.

hit the mall. And we didn't leave until they were locking up the place. For nearly twelve hours, girlfriend searched high and low for the perfect outfit, but nothing seemed right. After running in and out of damn near every store, and listening with a sympathetic ear to her constant complaints of how loose everything fit, I was beginning to get frustrated—and famished. But her perky ass kept urging, "Just one more store," and "What do you think of this one?" I was about ready to check her into Undernourished Anonymous but tried to remain supportive—that is, until she turned and asked, "Does this dress make me look fat?" That was it. Game over. Why did she have to go there? "What's wrong with looking fat?" I snapped. "F.A.T. is fine. F.A.T. is fantastic. F.A.T. is about to get your ass smacked." Realizing she'd just insulted me, girlfriend tried to play it off: "Mo'Nique, girl, you aren't F-A-T fat, you're P-H-A-T, phat." Good save. She got that one right. I am Pretty, Hot, And Thick (P.H.A.T.). Her feeble attempt was enough for me to accept her apology and think that we'd gotten over that first awkward hurdle. But there would be more during our shopping day together.

Finally she settled on a little black minidress with spaghetti straps that was cute, but girlfriend didn't have the proper curves to wear that dress like a *real* woman. "Okay," I said. "Now, run over to Lane Bryant with me." You'd have thought I asked this woman to commit a murder, turn over her first-born—EAT. All at once, her demeanor changed. She got edgy. Agitated. This damn girl broke out in a cold sweat. "What about Macy's, instead?" she suggested. "I saw a sexy skirt about five hours ago in the window at Lane Bryant," I asserted. With a halfhearted laugh, girlfriend mumbled, "Mo'Nique, I'm sorry, but I don't want anyone to see me in there." I couldn't believe this rickety bitch said—after I'd run through the mall with her, mind you—that she didn't want to be caught in Lane Bryant. She might as well have added, "with your FAT ass," because at that moment it became clear. This wasn't a friend. In fact, on Mo's Thin-O-Meter, this one was an evil ten with an agenda. As long as her frail ego was stroked, and it was all eyes on her, shit was fine, but the moment the focus shifted, she couldn't handle it. My first thought—after should I head to the food court to cool off— was to smack her little ass right in the middle of the mall. But I remained cool, walked toward the store, and refused to let this evil one's attitude ruin my shopping day, or get my BIG ass left at the damn mall. This time, she was in the driver's seat. Realizing she'd just offended me again, she reluctantly entered the store, apologized for the verbal faux pas, and offered to help. With one skinny bitch in tow, what was the first voice I heard? Yep, you guessed it—an even skinnier salesgirl. You'd think we'd be able to escape the hungry in our own shops, but damn it, they're everywhere. Now, I was in no mood to be fucked with, and I ignored Olive Oyl when she asked if she could be of assistance. But skinny persisted—and proceeded to follow me around, eager to make a sale. Finally, after searching in vain for someone FLUFFY, I explained that I was in search of the perfect party outfit. "I've got it," her perky ass chirped as she dashed off. But she obviously didn't get it, because when she returned it was with a long-sleeved purple turtleneck and a matching floor-length skirt— WRONG! My so-called friend, in an attempt to make good, got in on the act, too. But this tag team didn't do anything but piss me off even more. Clearly, they were both confused, so I attempted to make it clearer: "Look, it must be strappy, plunging, short, and sexy." This time, girlfriend glanced at the salesgirl and mumbled, "Sexy?" She snickered, and the sales-

Before I was a Queen of Comedy,
I was a full-figured model at the age of eighteen.

girl snickered, too. That was it. Strike three. Time for me to count both of these skinny bitches out, and the salesgirl was up first.

Now, I'm not one to discriminate, but why should the skinny be allowed to work in stores that cater to the FULL-FIGURED? You don't see too many FAT girls behind the counter at BeBe and Express, do you? I didn't think so. Bony bodies can't appreciate our curves, in, say, a string bikini (oh, and I look marvelous in one, by the way), or understand how to dress flat-out feminine curves because they don't have any. Women aren't all the same shape, so it would be nice to find looks that flatter individual shapes, rather than to force women to change to suit the clothes. That's also why dressing the CURVY only works if someone that looks like us is assisting us, and why I told this wiry woman to "go over to BeBe or Banana Republic and give a BIG girl a shot at selling clothes to me." She was speechless, but I wasn't done yet. While sashaying my BIG ass out of that store, I finished with, "The only thing a skinny saleswoman can do for me is point me to a F.A.T. one, because that's who's getting my money."

These two—and millions of others—believe that F.A.T. folks should just accept whatever retailers try to hand us. Let me tell you something—Mo'Nique has never accepted things "just because," and damn it, I never will. HEFTY honeys, you shouldn't either. To prove a point—and defend the honor of PORTLY PLAYAS—this crazy coworker of mine needed to learn a lesson, too. But I'm not gonna reveal how our shopping spree ended. Read on to see how I got even with that skinny, frontin'-ass bitch in chapter 5, "Once You Go Fat." Because you know payback's a bitch, and I had to teach this one a lesson.

That day at the mall taught me a lesson. I was just one of

the millions of BIG girls who has popped, ripped, torn, busted through, and broken her fair share of poorly constructed clothes just to be fashionable, or resorted to muumuus in defeat. On the road, during my stand-up shows, I notice SHAPELY sisters in my audiences all covered up, and it hurts my feelings to know that you aren't being the vibrant, sexy women that you can be. When I see you suffocating and covered in black from head to toe, it tells me that you've given up—and in—and are ashamed of your body, and that's not cool. Stretch marks are nothing to be ashamed of—something to camouflage, maybe, but definitely nothing that should stop the fashion show. Mornings shouldn't start out depressing because there's nothing fashionable in your closet. Because just like other women, sizable sisters want to feel confident in every area of their lives, too, in outfits that have words like Lycra, stretch, and spandex. (While we're on the subject of spandex, I must speak on black leggings for a moment. This is another case of everything not being made for every body. Cellulite ain't an attractive thing. Hey, we've all got it, but that doesn't mean everybody wants to see it. For some of you, this may present a problem because stretch pants have become *the* staple of your wardrobe. This is your girl, Mo'Nique, giving it to you straight. Damn it, BIG girls, stay the hell out of stretch pants if your thighs make them look like cottage cheese. Shit, you've got to have some shame, please.) I know, you've also got to have some options, and that's about to change with Mo'Nique on the fashion scene.

BIG girls, there's no reason why we should still be subjected to ugly clothing. If I have my way, soon your wardrobe worries will be a thing of the past, especially when Mo'Nique's Fashions hits the market. That's right! I'm going for classy clothing for the CHUNKY but FUNKY in sizes fourteen to thirty-two. My line will celebrate the beauty of the body in *all* its abundant glory. Get ready for hip, sexy gear that's tasteful, comfortable, and yes, ladies, affordable. It's for those who want to be stylish—in daring denim, fox-trimmed wool blends, marvelous minks, jammin' jumpsuits, and velvet capes and coatdresses—but don't want to starve to do it. They may say, "Oh, no she didn't . . ." That's when you reply, "Oh, yes I did, and I look damn good in it." Every time you step out—like when we filmed *The Queens of Comedy*, and I stepped onstage in a two-piece gold-and-tomato-red leather pantsuit with splits up the legs and a red bustier—look great doing it. That became my motto long before I landed my television show. The first thing I told producers—after they told me how much money they were gonna pay me—was not to have Nikki wear muumuus and sit around the house all day. She must go out on dates, have adventures, boyfriends, and as much sex as possible. Thankfully, they understood my desire to make a statement with this character and agreed with everything—except the as-much-sex-as-possible request. Now, along with my girl, Yvette Wilson, who plays my best friend, Andell Wilkerson, on the show, we're making television history as two THICK honeys that look good and dress well. We're also making the BOLD statement that sexy in Hollywood doesn't always mean a size two. This time, it's a twenty-two. America believes it, too, because *The Parkers* has consistently remained number one among African-American households since the first season. THANK YOU, AMERICA! THANK YOU, B.I.G. GIRLS! I LOVE YOU! I also love that what you see each week is pure Mo'Nique. They just changed my name to Nikki Parker and let me roll. And you won't catch Nikki rolling up on *Jerry Springer*, especially with topics like "You're Too Fat to Wear That." Shows like

The beehive hairdo may have been all the rage in the sixties, but I was determined to bring it back in the eighties. I'm not smiling because my neck is sore from sleeping cute to keep all that hair perfectly placed.

those are exploitative and do nothing to champion the CHUBBY cause. That's why we've got to be well dressed whenever we step out of the house, and why you can't rely on the opinions of the skinny. A skinny evil one will have you walking around looking crazy all day just so she'll stand out.

There are ways to stand out and be elegant at 300 pounds, but the only way you'll be able to tell what those pounds look like is if retailers begin to make dressing rooms LARGE enough to accommodate us. Trying to get through the doorways of some of these four-by-two cells is like trying to get five THICK chicks in a Hyundai—it ain't gonna work, I don't care who gets in first. Shit, by the time you wrestle open the door and get your clothes and purse in, you've got to sit down and catch your breath, and even that can be a problem because half the time, only half of our asses fit in those petite seats. And forget about seeing all of yourself in those skinny dressing-room wall mirrors, because that ain't happening either. Once I was having such a problem that a saleswoman asked if I wanted to go into the handicapped room instead. HELL NO! I'm not handicapped. I'm FAT. That's why stores with common dressing areas where folks just grab a spot and disrobe get my vote. You can spread your shit out and observe all of yourself in floor-to-ceiling mirrors from every angle. But it never fails. I'm minding my business, and a skinny bitch wearing a Victoria's Secret thong right next to me gives me a smug grin because she thinks her ass looks better than mine in that little strip of fabric. Imagine how her grin turns to a frown when my pants come off, and I've got mine on, too. Check the enemy every chance you get, even half dressed in a fitting room. But I must give props where they're due. Lane Bryant has really stepped up the game with sizable dressing rooms, mirrors that accommodate ALL of us, and chairs that

Meditating in my hotel room before my first appearance
on *Def Comedy Jam* in New York. Check out the hair,
even with a warm-up suit on, it was always laid.

are LARGE enough to seat BIG asses comfortably. They've also widened the aisles so we can get through them and see what's what.

Now, if Lane Bryant only made shoes. The right shoes can make or break an outfit. That's why yours have got to say style, class, and sophistication. But finding the proper pair of kicks that won't have your feet so stuffed in, as Chris Rock says, that it looks like two loaves of bread baking, can be tough—though not impossible. With a little effort, the help of a reputable shoemaker, and a sturdy pair of reinforcements, fashion-forward sisters who are size elevens can rock the cute winter boots and the stylish summer sandals, too. But not if you haven't taken care of your tootsies, ladies. Toes can be sexy, but not if they've been cooped up too-tight cheap shoes. That's why you've got to treat your feet sweet with pedicures that'll leave your digits suckable. Some of us are carrying a HEAVY weight, so it's important for our feet to look great. Ditto for our legs. I treasure mine, and when they're attached to a sexy pair of stilettos, men do too. The same goes for frilly underwear. Say so long to Victoria's Secret because the real secret is that Victoria isn't interested in putting BIG asses in lacy bras and panties. But like everything else, a little creative redesign gets you around that, too.

You may not have to be an expert redesigner much longer, because things finally appear to be changing. Last year Lane Bryant kicked off New York's Spring Fashion Week with a standing-room-only intimate apparel show. And designers are beginning to incorporate LARGER sizes into their fashion lines. Shit, they've got to if they want to stay in business. There are countless Internet plus-size fashion Web sites, and women across America—like one fed-up fourteen in Los Angeles who walked into a discount store and found maternity clothing in the plus-size department—are getting proactive, too, and demanding management move it. So, CURVY girls, love your proportions—even if they're HUGE. And stop wasting time worrying about a few extra pounds. Shit, with all the girdles, Wonderbras, and slimming slips out there today, just rearrange your shit and keep on steppin'. When folks try to dictate what the perfect body *should* look like, strut your stuff like the DIVA that you were born to be and tell them they're looking at it. Begin to define yourself as more than just your body and experiment with looks that flatter and play up what you've got, because that's really what counts. Sexy is more than a size—it's a destination. And for some of you, the journey will be long, but necessary. However, if along the journey you happen to find yourself stuck at the mall with a bunch of skinny women, and you're at your wit's end, don't go crazy. Drive them crazy, instead. When you love you, it's easy—and fun—to break the rules, and thumb your nose up at society's rigid beauty standards. Mo'Nique says, WEAR WHATEVER THE HELL MAKES YOU FEEL SWELL. But whatever you do, and however you do it, damn it, you better do it with S-T-Y-L-E.

Mo's Guide to the Best & Worst Designers

If you're F.A.T. and desire fabulous fashions, forget these designers. They'll just hurt your BIG feelings.

CALVIN KLEIN   He makes clothes only a child could love.

TOMMY HILFIGER   Maybe one day "he'll figure" out a way to incorporate a few fourteens, sixteens and twenties in his clothing line.

VERSACE   Too bold. Too bright. Too damn much for F.A.T. girls to get away with.

GUESS!   Guess they don't plan on two-digit dames sporting that little emblem.

BABY PHAT   Love ya, Russell. But damn, can BIG girls get some love too?

DESIGNERS THAT RESPECT THE CURVES

Lane Bryant

Salon Z, Saks Fifth Avenue

Just My Size

Avenue

Ashley Stewart

Marina Rinaldi

Eileen Fisher

Ashanti

Ronda's Boutique (Baltimore)

Torrid (Los Angeles)

Frederick's of Hollywood

F.A.T. Girls' Survival Tips

SHOPPING

* Only shop with other BIG girls.

* Hit the food court frequently for energy.

* If they don't have it in your size, buy two and sew them together.

FIVE

Once You Go Fat . . . Baby!

THE REAL WOMEN MEN WANT

THERE WAS ONCE A TIME, not so long ago, when skinny bitches didn't respect BIG girls, especially when it came to men. If a F.A.T. girl walked into the club and thought she had it goin' on, the skinny didn't even turn around. They were so arrogant and so damn confident that their men would NEVER look our way that they kept right on doing what they were doing. At the beach, they sported dental floss bikinis and strutted their stuff proudly, sure no man would want to see a F.A.T. girl in a thong. And they didn't even bother to block if we attempted to give a fine man our number. They just laughed. On that rare occasion when a man did happen to step out of line, glance in our direction, or start to act shady, the slim didn't fret, they just batted an eyelash or showed a cunning smile, and if that didn't work, they'd show a little skin and flirt openly. Back in the day, that evil shit worked. But, thank you, Jesus, those damn days are gone.

Skinny bitches, get nervous; your worst nightmare has come true. That's right, the game is finally changing. No more booty calls at three o'clock in the morning, no more refusing to be seen with us in public, and no more bringing takeout to the house because he's embarrassed by our hearty appetites. Today, MEN ARE CHECKIN' FOR BIG GIRLS, especially from September to March, when it's cold outside. Oh, it may have taken a while, but men have finally realized that in the dead of winter, the last thing they want sleeping next to them is a skeleton. They'd much rather spoon with a F.A.T. girl who can smother them with love, then smother them some pork chops. And I'll let you in on a BIG secret: once a man goes F.A.T., he ain't never goin' back. Shit, he won't want to, because BIG-girl lovin' is so damn good, he'll wonder why he didn't go F.A.T. sooner.

As much as I despise the ways of skinny women, I've got to hand it to them, they know how to reel men in—by demanding million-dollar mansions, condos in the Caribbean, and sports cars. But they don't have a clue about how to keep men on the hook—by getting their name added to the deed. It takes more than showing some skin to get in. You better show some cooking skills and some bedroom tricks, too. Because in this day and age you can't just up the ante and not up the panties.

So for those poor misguided souls who think FATTY girls are at home starved for love and affection, who assume that all we do is lie around the house all day stuffing our faces with popcorn, depressed because we don't have that someone special, keep right on thinking that stupid shit, but I've got news for you. F.A.T. WOMEN KEEP MEN, plenty of them. In fact, skinny girls, do you know where your man is right now? He just might be at home with us. That's right. TONS (pun

SKINNY WOMEN ARE EVIL 121

intended) of BUXOM beauties have men at the house waiting on them hand and fat-ass foot. Hell, some of the best relationships are between BIG-as-a-house women and the skinny men who love them. And if you think I'm kidding, ask around. Better yet, ask men. Shit, my uncle Billy and aunt Vera have been married for more than thirty years. He'll tell you a petite woman is a waste of time. First off, they don't ever venture into the kitchen, which means most of them don't know the difference between a strainer and a container. Sex is a pain rather than a passion. In the heat of a good romp, a man wants some cushion for the pushin', or at the very least something he can grab on to—like an ass. And, forget about housekeeping skills—they don't have them. Shit, pull up to the house without calling, and chances are, it's so damn dirty, even the roaches are running out screaming, "Help, we're hungry." Girl, you might be cute, but you still gotta know how to be a woman. And a *real* woman knows how to cook, clean, and make a man scream. Maybe if they'd play fair, instead of being so damn evil, we could teach them a few things.

The thing is, some of them know their shit is shaky. That's why a BIG girlfriend who still associates with the enemy reported that an evil eight masquerading as a cool one asked her our secret for keeping a man hooked. Instead of treating this hard-up heifer like the enemy that she is, BIG girl told her our number-one secret: We cook for our men. That's right, COOK. You know the old saying, "The way to a man's heart is through his stomach?" That shit is true. It's also the route you take to get to his wallet, and to get your name on the deed, too. But they don't think long-term. It reminds me of a skinny girl back in Baltimore who wanted to impress her boyfriend. She was a career woman and wasn't interested in mastering the art of cooking; she was more of a fine-dining

Ronda Bell, Jesse Jackson, and me at a political fund-raiser.

expert, but she'd lied to her man for so long that eventually her back was against the wall, and she had to prepare him a home-cooked meal. So she asked around and found a chef to whip up a gourmet meal. Instead of sticking around and picking up a few tips, girlfriend went upstairs and took a bath so she'd be ready when he walked through the door, while the chef prepared the table and left out the back door. When her man got home, girlfriend took the credit for everything. And I'm not mad at her. Sometimes you've got to take matters into your own hands—but use some common sense. She was so busy getting dolled up that she didn't write anything down, so when her man asked a few key questions, like can you make this again tomorrow night? and the chef wasn't available, her conniving ass didn't have a clue. That's the kind of silly shit skinny women do. Now a BIG girl like me would have taken advantage of this opportunity to learn from a professional and written down every ingredient. Then, after dinner, my man and I could have bathed together. Learn to *really* cook and perform wild, passionate sex—and not necessarily in that order—and you'll have a man hooked for life.

That's why, for the life of me, I can't understand why evil ones don't get it, or why they won't unite with the ones who really know what time it is. See, ladies, when it comes to relationships, we're more practical, more open, more willing to handle all of our mate's needs. Sure, we like to dine out, but fuck a five-star restaurant when Costco's got steaks two for twenty, and it's cold outside. We can hook up a couple of T-bones with all the trimmings and eat in. And after slaving over a hot stove, you won't hear us say, "Honey, I made it all for you to enjoy." No, sir. We're going to sit down and enjoy that dinner right along with our man, right after we've gotten his house shoes and asked about his day. When dinner is done, we'll partake of some strawberry shortcake with whipped cream and carry that can of Redi-Whip right on into the bedroom for a sticky romp. And when all of that is through, if that man wants to have a smoke or a smoked ham sandwich, we've got that covered, too. That's because good women anticipate their man's needs long before he even knows he needs anything.

But try telling that pearl of wisdom to giraffes who spend countless hours agonizing over how their hair looks, whether their skirt is short enough, and should it be a G-string or thong. Listen up: First, men don't care about hair. As long as you whip the sex on him right, you could be as bald as Michael Jordan. Second, if your skirt is tight and your ass is too, who cares about length? And third, answer the door butt-naked, and points one and two won't matter one bit. BIG girls stress over less self-centered concerns, like, is the refrigerator stocked with enough of his favorite beer? Did we fry enough chicken, make a big enough pot of collard greens, and will two sweet potato pies do? And, most important of all, how long is it going to take to cook all this food, so it's hot when he comes home from a hard day's work? See ladies, aside from being FLABULOUS, we know how to make a man feel like a king.

And after putting in twelve hours on the job, what a king desires most is a queen who understands the three F's: he wants to be fed, fucked, and flattered. Shit, master the three F's, and he'll rush home every Friday with paycheck in hand and your favorite snack to go along with it. And you don't have to look like Halle Berry to receive the royal treatment, or to find the love of your life, because lasting love is about more than what a woman looks like. It's about what she's made of, too. Which means that we don't all have to be fashion-model thin to snag good men. In fact, Los Angeles, California, is probably the only place on earth where men prefer knitting needles to hourglasses.

That's why I love the South. You definitely can't miss the curves on THICK sisters down there. They should call Hotlanta B.I.G.-girl capital of the world because in Georgia, slim women may be getting free drinks, but they damn sure ain't getting the phone numbers and dinner dates. It's the F.A.T. honeys who're mixin' it up at the Martini Bar in Midtown, licking ice cream cones at Phipps Plaza in Buckhead, and tailgating to upscale soul-food joints like Sylvia's, Justin's, and for late-night bites, Gladys Knight's House of Chicken & Waffles. And please, don't mention the D word down South, unless it's doughnut, and it better be Krispy Kreme. Diet isn't even part of their vocabulary unless it's a SEE-FOOD diet. Oh yes, it's a different world, and CURVACEOUS cuties are getting plenty of action with the extra POUNDS they're packing. Back in the day, if a man brought a F.A.T. friend home to meet his mama, it was a sign of success, wealth, and a marriage made of marvelous meals. In some areas of the country, it's still a good idea to show up with a THICK one, especially if Mom lives in Chicago and it's the middle of December. A mink coat may be marvelous, but underneath that mink, girlfriend better have a pair of FAT feet, FAT arms, and a FAT belly, too, just to walk down Michigan Avenue, or the hawk (for those of you unaware, that's a fierce wind) will snap her little ass like an icicle.

And speaking of snapping, get the wrong frail female in bed, and depending on the position, you could mess around and puncture a lung, or fracture an arm, or knock her little ass against the headboard too hard and wind up a murder suspect. You see, rather than go with the flow, the tiny constantly go against it. I guess you would, too, if you lacked the necessary

Okay, I know you're thinking, the plaid with the white stockings
isn't working. Well, standing in front of a giant ring with Michael Lee at
sixteen years old, you couldn't tell me I wasn't stylin'.

meat to keep it together when it counts. Ladies, a man may say he wants a woman who's 36-24-36, but, in the heat of a good sex session, only if she's five-three. Trust me, "Ooh, you're crushing my kidney," or, "Stop, you're bending my leg too far back" is not the type of pillow talk he wants to hear, and he never will with a BIG girl between the sheets. The only response he'll get is, "Boy, stop crying. Just hold on, I got you." That's because we treat gettin' busy as an adventure and are prepared to handle this quest any way you want to bring it. So, bring a pair of rock climbing boots, a hard hat, and a Bible, because you're gonna need to pray that you make it through. Oh, and don't forget to pack a snack for two, because when I call for a break, it's sandwich time.

When you're BULKY, sometimes half the fun of having sex is coming up with a few new tricks. In fact, my man calls me the F.B.I.A.—the Freakiest Bitch in America. So, trust me, you will never read in the *National Enquirer* that Mo'Nique lost her husband because she wouldn't get busy. (Now, you might read that back in the day, I lost one to an old assistant. But that one wanted to be a BIG girl, anyway, and trust me, that's another story you don't want to hear.)

I like stories and songs that tell it like it is. Take that sexy crooner, Maxwell, for example. He told his woman he'd do whatever, wherever, whenever. That's my motto, too. And Babyface's "Whip Appeal." I know he was singing that one to us. Any man that tells you he'll pay your bills, buy your clothes, and cook dinner, too, as soon as he comes home from work, has a BIG sister on his mind. See, for a man like that, I'll do anything. So if he feels like breaking a headboard, brother, you ain't said nuttin' but a word, let's do it. Try a new position? Just let me know if I'm on top or not. Because sexual experimentation is fun, and great sex—like a good all-you-can-eat buffet—feeds the soul. That's why, when we find good lovin', we'll do anything to keep it coming—literally.

But, let me tell you one no-no. Sex with a FAT man. BIG brothers, I love you, keep right on eating, but just know that Mo'Nique can't get with you. Because when you've got ten toes up, and ten toes down, two FAT asses in the bed rollin' around just doesn't work. I've tried it, and baby, it's too damn much going on. He's looking for my shit, I'm lifting his gut to find his, and neither one of us can breathe. We're both tired as hell before we've even gotten busy. That's why there are certain spots you can hit on a BIG girl and never touch the "secret garden." When you're tired, the chin, under the arm, the double layer of stomach, and the front of the thighs are just a few of the key spots that'll get him in—and off—without a lot of work. And, for you ladies with FAT ankles, use 'em. Shit, you name it, and if I can contort my body, I'll definitely give it a shot. Don't frown. When you're in a committed relationship, you commit to doing it any way he wants it. And believe me, skinny girls, if you won't, there's a BIG girl who probably will. So lose the inhibitions before you lose your man, and remember, the more you know, the better it goes. But let me make one thing perfectly clear. This only applies to a good man who's treating you like a Queen.

The more you sweet-talk a man, the more goodies he's liable to throw your way. If the penis is the size of a number-two pencil, scream like it's the BIGGEST pencil you've ever seen. He might not be able to cook worth a damn, but act like those tough-ass ribs are the best damn thing this side of Texas. And maybe he is a five-minute brother—shit, scream for ten. Lord knows I should've won Emmys for some of my past performances because men love to have their egos—and everything else—stroked, and if that's what it takes to keep the million-dollar mansions, the condos in the Caribbean, and the brand-new Benz in the driveway, then damn it, what a small price to pay. There are some F.A.T. sisters married to professional athletes, living in PHAT mansions, and how do you think they got there? Not by playing games. They got there because BIG girls are like Avis—WE TRY HARDER. And brothers appreciate that.

But the scrawny aren't cut out to flatter, they'd much rather be flattered—constantly. And they're selective, too. They only select the men who have money—and are willing to spend all of it on them. And they love to keep a few good men around to do with whatever they want. Like that crazy Nola Darling from Spike Lee's film *She's Gotta Have It*. Here was a woman with three men—a sensitive type who wanted to settle down with her; a narcissistic model who only saw her as his trophy; and an aggressive man who made her laugh. But who did her crazy ass end up with? None of them. Why, because her skinny ass was confused. Why was she confused? Because she was starving the entire movie. It's a scientific fact that you can't think clearly on an empty stomach. That's why Nola couldn't decide which one she wanted to settle down with, so in a hungry haze, she let them all go. BIG girls don't get down like that. While the skinny like to get hooked up with gourmet meals, we, on the other hand, love to go into that kitchen and hook a man with a meal. No one demonstrated that better than my girl Loretta Devine in Terry McMillan's film *Waiting to Exhale*. It's one of my all-time favorite movies. You remember the scene where girlfriend strolled across the street and introduced herself to the new neighbor, Gregory Hines? After getting the facts—that he was a lonely widower—Loretta sashayed those heavenly hips back across the street so Gregory could see just what he could be

My play brother Vernon and me before one of my performances.

getting, then went home and put the BIG-girl plan into action. After whipping up a sinful soul-food dinner, she brought it back over to that man, helped him fix up his house, and by the end of the movie, who was getting busy? The F.A.T. girl, that's who. Whitney, Lela, and Angela may have been getting laid, but they still didn't have one stable relationship. Want to know why? You guessed it. None of them could cook. Angela was so busy burning shit outside the house that if she had brought her skinny self back in and burned in the kitchen, he never would have left, although he was a shortie, and I've got my own theory about that—but we'll get to that later. Whitney was worrying with a meddling mama and a man who wouldn't commit. Maybe if she'd committed to setting the table instead of the bed, she would have snagged that man. And Lela, that poor child didn't have a clue what to do with the men coming her way. When she got into the fight with one suitor and he started throwing oranges at her on the balcony, a sensible sister would have taken a few of those oranges and made a fabulous fruit salad, but not this one. She threw them right back. And when she had BIG boy chasing after her, what did she do? Daydreamed about the future. Girlfriend missed the fact that all she needed to do was hook that BIG rascal up something sweet to eat. I'm telling you, cooking skills—or lack thereof—explain a lot. Like why some skinny ones are so damn evil. Shit, you'd be evil too, if your stomach growled constantly and you didn't want anyone to know what was really going on—that you AIN'T GETTING SHIT! That's right. There are a lot of sexually frustrated women out there who've got N-O-T-H-I-N-G going on. I've gotten reports from the TUBBY troops, and the C word is being tossed around a lot lately in skinny circles. You know the C word, *celibacy*. That's some shit the skinny invented.

And men are tired of jumping through hoops for women who play games—like that three-month rule game. Listen, most women know within five minutes if they're "feelin' " a man enough to sleep with him. And though we don't want to give it up the first night, waiting three months (until you "supposedly" get to know someone) still doesn't guarantee he'll stick around. I knew a girl who had a fine man in love with her. So fine, in fact, she'd go to sleep every night with a pillow between her legs just thinking about how she wanted it to be him. But she didn't want to go there, so she convinced herself—and that man—that they should wait ninety days, like that's some magical gauge that makes it okay to get busy. During that time, she had him jumping through hoops, trying to impress her. But eighty-five days into it, girlfriend got a call from the former love of her life, who had returned to town. It was always their understanding they'd be together. TMI—TOO MUCH INFORMATION. Men are goal-oriented. Don't give them dates, unless it's the date you plan to give them some. This fine man got played, and it wasn't based on getting to know him. It was based on getting something better. See, my three-month rule is different. If after three months a man hasn't sufficiently done his job (and it's my job to determine what that is), it's *my* prerogative to let *him* go. You don't just automatically get all this loveliness for time served. But wouldn't you know it, this dumb girl let the good one go, and the one she was saving herself for returned to inform her that he was engaged—to another woman that he slept with the first night. Why waste time on a maybe when you can have a suitor for each season? A good man in the winter, a roughneck in the spring, a corporate brother in the summer, and by fall, fall madly in love with the right one.

Finding true love takes work, and that's something most folks don't realize until they've had a few bad relationships. And trust me, I've had my fair share of relationships that started out great and evolved into physical fights. Though it wasn't funny at the time, I had to laugh to keep from crying. If you're reading this book, and that's the situation you find yourself in, then girlfriend, I'm talking to you. Sure, love is about pain, but it shouldn't come from a black eye or a busted lip. Before you can love anyone else, you've got to love yourself first, and believe that it will get better. That's what happened for me. But getting to happiness was an emotional ride of pain before the joy.

My first husband was intelligent, ambitious, and bad-tempered. We met in broadcasting school, started out as casual friends, and soon began dating. Did I also mention he was an amateur boxer? That probably should have been my first clue that we'd end up in the ring someday, but when you're young and in love, you do stupid shit—like marry a man after your grandmother says there's something about his eyes she doesn't trust. There was drama from the start, but it wasn't bad enough to walk away, even though he threw bowls at me, spat in my face, and shook me. Through it all, believe it or not, I thought I could fix the situation. That's right, I was a fixer. Soon our son arrived, and things only got worse. He assumed that my job would be to stay home and care for our son, but I wanted to become a comedienne. This difference of opinion often led to some knock-down, drag-out fistfights. And boy, could he pack a punch. But you don't just hit a BIG girl and that's the end of it. I got my licks in, too. Damn near KO'd his ass a couple of times. The police were called to our home so much that eventually we ended up before a judge who warned him that if she saw him in her courtroom again,

Don't we make a cute couple. This is Dorien Wilson and me as our characters, Nikki Parker and Stanley Oglevee. The reason he's smiling so much is because deep down inside, he knows he wants me.

he'd go to jail. But it didn't take long for more battles to ensue. It had always been an above-the-neck fight until he got me with a kidney blow. That's when I knew it was time to go. So I packed up my baby and moved to Atlanta, where comedy was booming for black folks. There, I started a new life and concentrated on building a career. But our drama wasn't over. After serving eight months in jail, he showed up in Atlanta, ready for round two. There were times when he'd hit me, and then I'd hit the stage with a busted lip or a black eye, trying to tell jokes just to keep from crying. After crying to my family one too many times, my mother finally told me to come home. So I packed up again, got into the car, and was headed back to Baltimore, but before I even left the Georgia city limits, I considered going back to this fool, and even called home to tell my family I was going to give it another try. But my mother was serious and told me to be the woman she raised me to be and bring my ass home. So I climbed back into the car—mind you, it was a GEO Storm, so you know getting in and out of that little ride was a task—but my baby and I did it and never looked back. That seemed like the longest car ride of my life, but I realized then that I couldn't fix him. Folks have to do that for themselves. I'm just glad I can talk about it now, because some sisters can't because they didn't survive the abuse.

I can't believe how blessed my life became after I took that first step. Once we settled back in Baltimore, my career thrived. I opened Mo'Nique's Comedy Club and performed nationally on *Def Comedy Jam* and *Showtime at the Apollo*. By the time my second husband came along, I was a local celebrity. We married after dating for three years. This time around the abuse was mental and Miss Fix-It was at it again, trying to help him get over emotional hurdles and losing myself in the process. And it was hard leaving this one because he moved clear across the country so I could make my dreams a reality. As much as I hated to end the marriage, it just got too heavy to bear. But it's okay. I'm clear about life now, and about how wonderful a healthy union can be. Perhaps you're asking yourself, What happened? Why did I abandon my belief that you should do all you can for your man? I didn't. But in addition to physical and mental abuse, these first two were short, and typically that ain't the only deficiency. Hell, a sister's got needs, and I needed to stop doing all the heavy lifting during sex. I like to be lifted sometimes, too, and shorties can't get the job done, so it was see you later, 'bye.

In between marriages, I found myself back on the dating scene, and damn it, I was rusty. I know it can be difficult, and a bit scary, to expose yourself and your imperfections to strangers, and I suspect that's what's stopping some of you, my fine, FLUFFY sisters, from having truly happy relationships. Maybe you're shy. Don't be. Intimacy (read: sex) is just like riding a bike. Or perhaps it's a body issue. Girlfriend, don't allow a few extra pounds to stop you from getting the love you deserve. So what if your belly hangs over your belt. So do the bellies of half of the men in America. Never mind that your breasts hit the floor when the bra comes off. Channel the size two within and go get yours, girlfriend. Shit, we've all got flaws, but who's got time to stress over minor imperfections when you're sitting on a major masterpiece? I don't care if a man wants to take you around the corner for a cup of coffee, you better say yes, because the man of your dreams just might work in—or own—a Starbucks.

After dealing with my share of short men, I was smitten when a big strapping hottie that played for the NFL's Baltimore Ravens asked me out. There's nothing better than having a tall, well-dressed man on your arm, especially one that's eager to impress—and this one was. We went to a fancy French restaurant, the kind where a maître d' hands you the menu. Now, this was new for me, but so was dating a tall man. So I tried to act sophisticated, but he could tell I was lost, so he offered to order for me. I sat back and told him, "Do your thing, playa." He ordered the filet mignon for himself and the duck à l'orange for me. Then we settled in and got to know each other. He'd been in the league for three years, was from the South, and had just bought his first mini mansion. After dating his share of groupies and gold diggers, he was ready to settle down, get serious, and have a family. This one was saying all the right stuff, like, Baby, is that enough food? and do you want more dessert? The cool thing about dating a football player is that it's cool to eat as much as you want. However, when that duck à l'orange hit the table, I was a bit concerned. But that didn't stop me from getting my chow on anyway. The evening was going great. The conversation was wonderful, but when we got to the car, baby, that damn duck started to quack and bubble in my stomach—and it was traveling south. So I tried to tighten up and hold it in, but it just kept quacking. When we got to his car, the plan was to hold it in until we made it back to his place, but he was one of those slow-moving defensive tacklers, and before he could make it around to his side, some folks spotted him and asked for autographs. That shit took five minutes. I'm sitting in the car, trying not to let that duck go, especially with the windows rolled up. When he finally got in, I could tell he was really feeling good about himself. After all, he'd taken me to that fancy restaurant, ordered up a fabulous meal, and now it was payback time. He smiled. I smiled. He laughed. I laughed. He thought he was about to get busy. I thought I was about to bust. We rode in silence for a few minutes until I just couldn't hold it in any longer. I turned the music up real loud like the song on the radio was my all-time favorite jam, rolled the window down, and began to let that duck go. At first it sounded like a slow tire leak, *Sssssssssssssssssssss*. Then the aroma kicked in. After a few moments, he started to get a whiff of the duck and tried to play it off, but it was bad. I was just satisfied that that duck and I had parted ways. But he couldn't take it any longer, and with a scowl he said, "Daaaaammmmnnn, girl. Was that you?" "No," I said, "It's that damn duck you ordered me." Aggravated, he shot back, "That's just nasty." "It may be nasty," I countered, "but boy, do I feel better now." I assumed the duck disaster was behind us and was ready to go back to his place to continue the evening, but boyfriend dropped me off at home, and I never saw his TALL, sexy ass again. That's because I was putting on airs, frontin', playing the skinny-girl game. He was a BIG country brother, which meant that I should've fried up a batch of chicken and some rice and gravy, invited him over, and then tackled him like it was Super Bowl Sunday. But I didn't, and I lost out. So take it from me, BIG girls, its best to stick to what you know because the dating game can be crazy like some of these females.

Women today give too much in relationships. Trust me, I'm speaking from experience. Remember, ladies, you're the queen. The one to be cherished. Before you get involved, investigate and ask questions. You just might find something you didn't expect—like a jail record. Sure, relationships are about give and take, but make sure you're taking just as much as you're giving. Ask yourself, What am I getting in return? If the answer is "nothing," then it's time to go. Shit, just because you're F.A.T. doesn't mean you should be treated like a door-mat. At the end of the day, when the makeup comes off and the Wonderbra stops working wonders, he's got to genuinely love you as much as you love him, rolls, dimples, and all. Don't settle just so that you can say you have a man. Go after what you want and believe that you're going to get it. I'm telling you, the next time around for me, he must be six-four, 280 pounds, and damn it, I must be able to ride him like a stallion. He's also got to be loyal, which is a rare quality in relationships these days.

Loyalty is definitely not a prerequisite for the skinny. They're only loyal to whoever's footing the bill. But not us—shit, we're there through THICK and thin. If a fight breaks out, we don't run and get help. We *are* the help. If there's a shoot-out, you better believe that extra roll of stomach FAT can stop a speeding bullet. Just kidding. But seriously, we'll knock a knucklehead out, so he can get away. And when it comes to my man, I ain't gonna fight you, I'm gonna kill you if you try to step to him. Like a certain intern who tried to cover for her man when the Republicans tried to step to him.

Now, it's no secret that presidents are notorious for keeping bimbos around to give them extra "secret services." That's just one of the perks of the job—to get all the sex they want in between (or during) cabinet meetings. But when news broke that Bill Clinton was caught in the middle of a sex scandal, folks were probably expecting to see another blonde as the president's latest conquest. But I knew from the circumstances—the BIG blue dress, the fierce desire to keep it all quiet, and the notion that she'd be Mrs. Bill Clinton one day—that this one was different. Monica Lewinsky fell hard for this southern boy from Arkansas. That's what got her. Shit, it would get me too, if I could get close enough. You've seen the way Bill crooned those Negro spirituals in Baptist churches, ate the hell out of some fried chicken, and sweet-talked the women. And when he left office, where did he move? HARLEM, USA. Shit, you can't get any blacker than that. Bill's past flings may have been with skinny bimbos trying to make a fast buck, but when he got with Monica, he got a girl who was in it for the love—and loyalty—of her man. She never intended to bring down the president of the United States, she just wanted to perform her duty as a loyal American—and got caught up in the process. And if you really think about it, this entire mess is Hillary's damn fault, because she knew how Bill was when she married him. She should have kept her eyes on her man. Shit, if Hillary had been loyal—and on her knees regularly—Monica's BIG ass never would have gotten near the presidential penis.

It's difficult to be loyal, though, when your name has been dragged through the mud. But, even in a breakup, there are proper ways of ending things. Take the enemy, for example: Instead of doing things rationally, they show up crying and out of control. They jack up the car, set your house on fire, and cause a scene in front of the entire neighborhood. And after they've done that, they're so worked up that they can't eat, can't sleep, break out in a fever, and act as if the entire world is about to end because it's all just too damn painful. Proving, once again, they're insane. But not us; that's too much damn work. You can break up with us if you want to, but it definitely won't go down at the house. It'll be after we've had you restock our entire kitchen, or at a five-star restaurant, over a four-course meal, and we'll be taking home three huge to-go platters as a parting gift. Shit, for some, breakups are when we do our best grubbin'—for free. Besides, men are just like buses. If you miss one, there's usually another one right around the corner with shinier rims.

But beware of the CHUBBY chaser who loves you

PLUMP, then wants to change you. Don't do it. Because BIG and beautiful is not an oxymoron. Plus, I'm happy with my thighs that rub together, my meaty arms, and my double chin, and I will not change them—or my mind—for any man. I had to get one straight when he asked if I ever considered a tummy tuck. I told him the only thing I'll be tucking is my blouse into my pants. Anyone who tries to get you to alter your appearance probably won't want—or recognize—you after you've done all that work, anyway. But that doesn't stop some crazy women from trying, or trying to please a man. I'm amazed at some of the works of art, or should I say freaks of nature, doctors have created in Tinseltown, the land of pop-on boobs, nose jobs, and Botox injections. I remember reading about one starlet who wasn't happy with her looks. She just had to have a set of BIG boobs. So she went to the best doctor in town, got an estimate, and got them done. A few weeks after the surgery, she discovered that one boob was larger than the other and, obsessed with trying to make it perfect, went under the knife again. After the adjustment she still wasn't satisfied and decided she needed a tummy tuck, face-lift, and Botox injections to go along with the new boobs. But after all that work, her husband left her for a small-breasted waitress from Ohio, and her lopsided ass was devastated.

And speaking of devastated. Remember that crazy coworker of mine, the one that dogged me through the mall? After our horrible shopping day together, I wasn't about to let this evil two get away, so I bet her that I could pull more telephone numbers than she could at the club that night. Of course she happily accepted my bet. But I had the upper hand, by knowing what she was wearing. Which meant that to win, I'd have to pull out all the stops. So I stopped by Frederick's of Hollywood (if you aren't familiar with FH, it's a trashy lingerie store) and picked up a black lace bustier and a fitted pair of slacks, and that night, IT WAS ON!

Girlfriend attempted to let her little black dress do the talking, sitting seductively at the bar with a chicken leg on display and an inviting smile. I, on the other hand, did it the BIG-girl way by eyeing a fine man, introducing myself in the buffet line, and casually mentioning that the Falcons were my favorite football team. Never mind that I didn't know a punt from a pass, a touchdown from a tackle. Shit, to score in this arena, all that's required are a few key phrases: seventy-two-inch BIG-screen TV, spread of hot wings, pizza, and kegs of beer. That's right. I bonded with these brothers over food, football, and my strategically placed cleavage. And that line of mackin' got me more drinks, telephone numbers, and dinner dates than this food connoisseur could handle.

But the truth is, it wasn't about the bustier—though that baby fit like a glove—it was about the woman inside it. I glanced over at my evil little friend, who attempted to work her scant black dress, but she just didn't have the goods or the talent to keep the interest of any of the men in the bar that night. Shit, these days, men want more than a pretty face. Beauty fades, but a woman he can laugh, cry, and eat with is a keeper. By the end of the evening, girlfriend was beaten at her own game, and Miss Size Two had to give this twenty-two her props. "Mo'Nique, how do you do it?" she wondered. "Men just love you." Now, that was the first accurate thing this crazy heifer had uttered all day. And I'm sure it probably took a lot for her to admit that a B.I.G. beauty had her beat. But I wasn't feelin' her, so my only advice was, "Food, and eating plenty of it, usually works." She looked sad, and for a moment I considered making amends with her malnourished ass. But after those two seconds passed and I

relived our horrible shopping day in my mind, I quickly
returned to my senses and realized that girlfriend wasn't sin-
cere—she was outdone. She could never handle being a BIG
girl. Like everyone else she only wanted the perks that come
along with all of this loveliness. I accepted her narrow ass, but
acceptance was a lesson she needed to learn on her own, and
I thought this club experience had driven that point home
when a HUGE platter of hot wings arrived at the table. She
claimed to have recognized the error of her evil ways and
vowed to never treat another BIG girl the way she treated
me. Then she stuck her hand out and called a truce on behalf
of skinny women everywhere. "We should work together to
trap, er, uh, to land good men," she urged. As a sign of soli-
darity, she picked up a wing, took a bite, and damn near
choked, but hey, it was a start. Finally, an evil two was becoming a cool two. But, just as we started to vibe, the finest
brother in the club looked our way and smiled. It was obvious
he was looking at me, and we flirted for a few moments
before he made his way to the table. But when he introduced
himself, this girl perked up, got smug, and reverted back to
her evil ways. Before I could put my chicken wing down, the
calculating bitch stuck her hand out, and her little leg came
from under the table, too. Then she introduced herself and
attempted to put the 34A's in this man's face. Edward (who I'd
met earlier that night) was polite and talked with her for a few
moments. And it didn't take long for her anorexic ass to
launch into the skinny-girl scheme—begging. "Boy, those
wings are so hot my mouth is on fire," she lied. I looked down
and noticed girlfriend had pushed the entire platter in my
direction, so it seemed like ALL the food on the table was
mine. So I sat back, polished off the rest of my wings and hers
too, and let girlfriend do her thing. After some small talk,

Edward turned to me and asked, "So, Mo'Nique, are we still on for Sunday?" Girlfriend's mouth dropped. She tucked that drumstick back under the bar when I said to the fine gentleman, "Why wait until Sunday?" He smiled, extended his hand, and we bid her adieu and left her at the club—alone. That's right. This time, I drove. But first I had to drive home the point that you will not drag me through a mall all day, insult me, attempt to take my man, and then expect me to act like things are cool. Payback's a bitch, and this evil one needed to be taught a lesson.

One lesson my mother taught me was to never leave girlfriends around my man. And never, under any circumstances, tell them how wonderful he treats you because some hard-up heifers will try to get treated, too, especially lonely bitter ones. BIG girls, I know you're excited to finally have someone to go to the movies with, laugh with, and eat with, but trust me, there are some who don't want to see you happy, and they're probably thin. Take a page from their book and don't say a word. When skinny women get new men, they show up wearing diamond rings and furs, and disappear at all hours of the day and night to spend time with their new man. They're so secretive, you don't even know they're dating anyone until it shows up in the tabloids, or on the news. I worked with a girl once, and she was like a clam. Whenever anyone asked her a question, she'd just give sneaky smiles, vacant stares, and one-word answers. So I thought, well, she is homely, ole girl probably doesn't have much going on. But a week later one of the music industry's hottest rappers was announcing his engagement, and who was sporting a FAT rock on her finger as his bride-to-be but this skinny, homely girl. That's why you can't trust them and why you can't throw a third party into the mix when it comes to your man. I did that once, with disastrous results. Don't get nervous. I'm not talking ménage à trois, I'm talking cleaning ladies.

When I landed the TV show, my Hollywood friends kept saying, "Girl, you're a star now. You need to get yourself a maid." It was never a luxury we could afford growing up. In fact, I never even considered hiring help until I moved into a big house and realized I didn't have the time—or energy—to clean up all those rooms. I thought, maybe they're right. Maybe I should get someone to come in and help out. After all, I am at the studio all day and on the road most weekends, and the last thing on my mind is cleaning a house. Shit, to tell you the truth, it's never ever on my mind. So I called one of those agencies and told them to send someone over. But I'll be damned if they didn't send over a perky little white girl. I called back and said, "Sorry, this one isn't going to work, send someone else." This time, it was a petite, cute black girl fresh out of college. I called back again and told them, "Excuse me, but you keep sending these cute young girls to clean up. I've got a husband, which means I need a sixty-year-old woman with one tooth and a single strand of hair and who doesn't speak a lick of English." That's exactly what they sent, and when she showed up, that didn't stop me from getting her old ass straight, too. "Look," I said in no uncertain terms, "when I grab my purse and coat, every one in the house needs to grab hers. Mama, that includes you, too." I felt bad making Mama and the maid wait outside, but there's only one queen in my castle—no exceptions.

And don't ask this queen to help you meet your king. I did that for the enemy once, and damn it, I'll never do it again. On the Thin-O-Meter scale, I thought this one registered a cool seven. In her twenties she ran in fast and crazy circles, dated fine men, and had a ball accepting pricey gifts from brothers who wanted to have a pretty face beside them when they stepped out. Now in her late thirties, and tired of the dating scene, she decided it was time to settle down, get serious, and start a family. She was also ready for someone who would love her unconditionally, and she asked if my husband had any eligible friends. When he asked her the type of man she liked, girlfriend launched into a laundry list of demands. "Well, he doesn't have to look like Denzel," she started. "But he should be at least six feet, have an athletic build, love motorcycles, and be a pit bull lover." Mind you, girlfriend hadn't had a date in three years, but damn it, she was still as picky as ever. What she should have said is, As long as he's breathing, he's a candidate. My husband decided to hook her up with a guy he played basketball with on weekends. So we made arrangements to meet at a sports bar to watch a Lakers play-off game. But, the week leading up to the big date, girlfriend bugged me with questions—what he looked like, what he did for a living, what kind of car he drove (all questions she could have asked him). When the evening finally arrived, we got to the place first. In anticipation of her arrival, he brought flowers and even made arrangements for her to enter the club through the VIP entrance. Thirty minutes after we arrived, she called to say she was stuck in traffic. An hour later she called with word that she'd just gotten in from work, wanted to freshen up, and would be there shortly. Two hours later, she finally showed up. When we introduced the two, he was in love, and she was in shock. Now, mind you, she didn't have a prospect to speak of, but she didn't want this one, either. And that's fine. Sometimes blind dates don't work out, but damn it, don't blame me for trying to do a good deed. And don't act like you can't enjoy a friendly outing and a free dinner. Instead of saying thank you, girlfriend complained about everything. She was allergic to the flowers, didn't like the location of the table because there was a draft, and couldn't find anything on the menu to eat (typical). Later, she accused us of trying to hook her up with someone she wouldn't be caught at a dogfight with, and then had the nerve to say she'd never speak to us again—and hasn't. But I'm glad her crazy ass is gone. Because though this man wasn't The One, she didn't know how to simply enjoy herself and go with the flow. That's why she's at home right now—by herself.

Well, I think I've made a compelling case for BIG girls and the reasons why we're the ones men *should* want. There's no such thing as the perfect relationship, and until the rebel forces recognize that fact, they'll continue to search in vain for the perfect mate. But it's the imperfections, the ebbs and flows, that make relationships special. So for the short time you're here, BIG girls, make your love goal one of balance and peace, the kind of peace that comes from knowing that you've truly found your soul mate—and the understanding that he or she may not arrive in the neat little package you expected, but in a nice, BIG box that you'll treasure for a lifetime.

Chubby Men We Like

* **Gerald LeVert,** singer

* **(The old) Al Roker,** *NBC Today Show* weatherman

* **Heavy D,** rapper

* **Mark McKewen,** *CBS This Morning* weatherman

* **Luther Vandross,** singer

* **Raymond Burr,** actor

* **William Conrad,** actor

* **John Belushi,** Actor

* **Barry White,** singer/composer

* **Fat Joe,** rapper

* **Big Pun,** rapper

* **Biggie Smalls,** rapper

* **Godfrey Cambridge,** actor

* **Fat Albert,** animated cartoon character

* **Jamal Mixon,** actor

* **Cedric the Entertainer,** comedian/actor

* **Fats Domino,** piano player

* **Louis Armstrong,** trumpet player

* **Martin Luther King III,** politician/civil rights activist

* **Fats Waller,** jazz pianist

* **William "The Refrigerator" Perry,** former football player

* **Rosie Greer,** former football player/minister
* **Reggie White,** former football player
* **Bruce Bruce,** comedian
* **Willard Scott,** *NBC Today Show* weatherman
* **(The Old) Al Sharpton,** Civil Rights Activist
* **Chris Farley,** comedian
* **Louie Anderson,** comedian
* **John Candy,** actor
* **W. C. Fields,** old-time movie star

BIG Girls Who've Got Flavor

* **Mo'Nique.** That's right. I'm at the top of the list. It's my damn book.
* **(The original) Oprah Winfrey,** talk show host, actress, philanthropist
* **Marilyn Monroe,** actress
* **Sophie Tucker,** singer
* **Kate Smith,** singer
* **Hattie McDaniel,** actress
* **(The old) Jennifer Holiday,** singer
* **Nell Carter,** singer/actress
* **Mary Lou Williams,** pianist/composer/arranger
* **Fannie Lou Hamer,** civil rights activist
* **Mahalia Jackson,** gospel singer

* **Mary McCleod Bethune,** educator

* **Kim Whitley,** actress/comedienne

* **Queen Latifah,** rapper/actress

* **Emme,** model

* **Jill Scott,** singer

* **Madame C.J. Walker,** businesswoman

* **Dorothy Height,** civil rights activist

* **Barbara Jordan,** politician

* **Star Jones,** attorney/TV show host

* **"Two Fat Ladies,"** cooking experts

* **Della Reese,** actress

* **Delta Burke,** actress

* **(The old) Kelly Price,** singer

* **(The old) Vesta,** singer

* **Roseanne,** comedienne

* **Rosie O'Donnell,** comedienne/actress

* **Anna Nicole Smith,** model

* **Lillian Russell,** singer/actress

* **(The old) Missy Elliott,** rapper

* **Ethel Merman,** singer/actress

* **Totie Fields,** comedian

* **Kathy Najimy,** actress

F.A.T. Girl Survival Tips:

DATING

* Prepare his favorite dinner regularly.

* If it's a first date and he's paying, order an appetizer, entrée, dessert, and to-go plate. You may not ever see him again, so get the most out of it.

* If he wants to break up, make sure it goes down over breakfast, lunch, or dinner.

Mo'nique's Top Ten BIG-Girl Jams

1. **"BRICK HOUSE" BY THE COMMODORES.** There's no way, when Lionel Richie sang, "The lady's stacked, that's a fact, ain't holding nothin' back, oh she's a brick house . . . ," that he could have had a skinny girl on his mind. Brickhouse was the Commodores' shout-out to BIG girls, so we'd know they wanted to get with us.

2. **"BABY GOT BACK," BY SIR MIX-A-LOT.** He may have been a one-hit wonder, but when Sir Mix-A-Lot told folks, "I like BIG butts and I cannot lie," he made it clear what's important in a *real* woman.

3. **"PASS THE COURVOISIER," BY BUSTA RHYMES.** Take a look at this video, and you'll know why it's one of my

all-time favorites. Hint: Check out the voluptuous, sexy, BIG girl beating Busta down in the alley. They say we look alike.

4. **"FATTY GIRL" BY LL COOL J, LUDACRIS, AND KEITH MURRAY.** It's about time those in the rap game paid homage to the real women they want between the sheets. Too bad they didn't give us our just due in the video, too.

5. **"SOUTHERN GIRL," BY FRANKIE BEVERLY AND MAZE.** Frankie Beverly knew how to get BIG girls on our feet, and not just down South, but also all over the world. This one is an anthem.

6. **"BIG GIRLS DON'T CRY," BY FRANKIE VALLI.** Baby, we ain't crying. We're partying. Because it's finally our time to shine.

7. **"IT'S RAINING MEN," BY TWO TONS OF FUN.** They may have each weighed a ton, but these FULL-FIGURED divas had "BIG voices to back it up. Whenever their jam came on in the club, everyone was on the floor.

8. **"LETS GET DIRTY," BY METHOD MAN AND REDMAN.** There's always a BIG girl representing in Red and Meth's videos, and that's why we like them.

9. **"RUMPSHAKER," BY TEDDY RILEY.** Now there's no way Teddy Riley could've been singing about anyone but BIG girls, especially since skinny ones don't have rumps to shake. It's about time BIG rumps got the recognition they deserve. Thank you, Teddy Riley, thank you!

10. **"PUMPS AND A BUMP," BY MC HAMMER.** Maybe if Hammer had gotten a few BIG girls to jump around with him, he'd still be on top of the game. But that's okay. He got it right with this ditty.

BONUS JAM: "EXCLUSIVELY," BY JILL SCOTT. Not just anyone can sing about food and sex in the same song and end up with a platinum CD. But my girl Jill Scott can and did— and I'm all for that. Go girl!

SIX

Exercise Is Overrated

WOES OF A HOLLYWOOD HEAVYWEIGHT

BIG GIRLS, I'VE GOT A CONFESSION. Throughout this entire book, I've talked, and at times even preached, about how wonderful it is to be a F.A.T. girl. How it's time BIG girls rise up, fight skinny evil ones, and claim our rightful place. I've given you examples of why the enemy needs to be destroyed, and even shared stories with you of how badly they've treated us and how my father told me, at a very young age, that I was the prettiest little (BIG) girl in the world. For years I carried myself like I was the shit, and was confident no one could outshine me. Yes, yes, y'all, I felt good about being 220 pounds. But baby, that loving myself F.A.T. shit flew right out the window the minute I hit Hollywood. That's right, ladies, I got out here and noticed that everyone in this crazy little town weighed ten pounds. And though I still kinda believed that BIG and BEAUTIFUL is not an oxymoron, for a year or so I lost my damn mind—and a hell of a lot of loot—trying to become a slimmed-down sister. I know you're probably saying to yourself, Oh no, Mo'Nique, not you, too. Damn it, yes, me, too.

What can I say? I got caught up in the L.A. way—of gyms that stay open around the clock, juice shops that are required morning stops for wheat grass served by the shot glass, and folks that take their workouts so seriously they have the telephone numbers to their nutritionists and trainers on speed-dial. Never before—and in no other city—has exercise played such an essential role in life. Out here, if folks don't get a good workout in, I pity the fool who has to deal with them. And I'm not talking jumping jacks. The exercises are strenuous stretches, but that doesn't stop them from enlisting in boot camp workouts, tae kwon do demonstrations, and paralyzing themselves with the latest kickboxing moves, all in the name of looking good. Some fitness fanatics can't start the day unless they've tackled a morning spin class, or go to sleep at night without stopping by the gym for a happy-hour workout. Perhaps the reason some are so obsessed with staying in shape is because, as they say, it never rains in southern California. And with the sun out eleven months of the year, and so much skin too, image is everything. It's nothing but tanned and pumped-up bods in the land of beautiful people—and damn it, I wanted to be one of them.

So for nearly a year I became a fitness-obsessed fool. But sisters, don't get it twisted. Becoming a twig was never the goal. My aim was to sculpt the MEGA-masterpiece God blessed me with into a well-toned temple, and though that meant sweating, I didn't necessarily want to kill myself to do it. So I found a way to get the job done without ever leaving the house, and with visions of the woman I was to become, rushed to the phone and ordered every piece of workout equipment known to man. First, the Ab Roller arrived. For

$59.99, this one, billed as the original abdominal exercise machine, promised a complete, no-nonsense workout and results in no time. But assembling that damn thing was a workout of its own. So was trying to figure out how the hell to do the Oblique Crunch, the Double Crunch, or the Raised Leg Oblique. And keeping the antislip power stand from slipping made me anti the Ab Roller. (Plus, it would've taken five years to ab all this flab.) Then, the Bowflex Ultimate arrived, and baby, this one was no joke. At a cost of $1,200, the Bowflex Ultimate called itself quite possibly the best home fitness machine ever made, with over ninety health-club-quality exercises and 410 pounds of resistance, rock-hard abs, sculpted legs, and a well-toned physique within reach in just six weeks, it sounded like a winner, but when that BIG box and those two thousand pieces got to the house, you needed six weeks or at least a Ph.D. in mechanical engineering just to figure out how to put that damn thing together. It was so complicated and frustrating that after the first few hours, it got tossed into the garage along with the Ab Roller, the NordicTrack, the Torso Track, the Suzanne Somers Toning System, and the Mini Stepper that arrived before it. Shit, even a slow treadmill moves too damn fast for me. When I attempted to raise the incline, the damn thing popped, sparked, and started to smoke. But there was no need to let a perfectly good fitness machine go to waste. Treadmills make the ideal clothes hangers. I've got one at home right now that has the skirt from last night, the blouse from last week, and a pair of pants from a month ago hanging right on it.

After weeks and not a sign of a toned body on the horizon, it was good-bye to workout machines and hello, exercise classes. That's right. When the Tae-Bo craze hit a few years

Los Angeles Laker Shaquille O'Neal is a good friend. When he made a
guest appearance on the show as himself, I dressed up as a trainer and
snuck in the locker room to get an autograph. This scene was so funny
that we could barely get through it.

Gale Alder/Paramount Pictures

ago, Billy Blanks made a guest appearance on *The Parkers*. If you've never heard of him, Billy's the exercise guru who developed a cardiovascular workout that combines martial arts kicks at a rapid pace that'll have your heart racing, pulse pounding, and sweat glands working overtime. After perfecting his unique brand of exercise, Billy took Tinseltown by storm and had housewives and Hollywood starlets alike raving about the difference in their bodies after a few short workouts. Tae-Bo became such a phenomenon that he went on to develop a series of workout videos and infomercials that have sold millions and tortured folks from Tijuana to Timbuktu. But I didn't get a taste of true Tae-Bo torture until after his appearance on the show. On the set, we did a couple of scenes where Nikki takes a class with her boo, Professor Oglevee, who's into it. The few choreographed moves we did didn't seem bad at all, so Billy invited me for a free workout at his studio. Since it was right down the street from the house, I decided to give it a shot. Somebody should have shot me for even thinking about setting foot in that insane asylum. After standing in a line that snaked around the corner, I finally made it into this crowded, hot little room. That's right. Folks out here stand in line to exercise. Shit, I'll line up to eat, I may even stand in line for a party, but I'll be damned if I'm gonna line up to sweat. But there I was, determined to give it a shot. Hell, I dropped twenty pounds just standing in this sauna. And this day Billy was nowhere to be found. Instead, it was some tiny female instructor in spandex shorts with a microphone wrapped around her head. While the regulars were getting into their usual spots, she was getting warmed up to kill us. But that didn't frighten the fanatics, it motivated them. Everyone was stretching and I thought about breaking out then, but was determined not to punk out. That is, until the music started. There was no warm-up. She just cranked the music, the entire class fell immediately into the Tae-Bo zone, and it was double-time for a solid hour. After five minutes of trying to get in step, I didn't care about trying to make it through. But getting out of there turned into survival of the fittest, with me against everyone in the room. See, with Tae-Bo, the entire class is moving in one motion, and you've got to keep up with the crazy instructor, kind of like doing the Electric Slide, except at a faster pace. Everyone was kicking and squatting simultaneously at fifty miles per hour. This stick of an instructor—and the fanatics following her—moved so fast, there was no way for me to break out, so I jogged in place instead. But that made them mad, because the F.A.T. girl was fuckin' up the flow. The fanatics glared at me as if to say, Either move it or move the hell out of the way. So, as soon as I could make it through this maze, I dashed out of that torture chamber and never looked back. By the time I made it to the car, I was swimming in sweat. When I got home, suddenly my BIG pool out back looked wonderful and refreshing. But there was just one problem: I didn't know how to swim. Hell, I don't know how to play the piano, either, but every BIG house I've seen has one sitting in the living room, and mine does, too. So I didn't let that minor technicality (or the fact that I was delirious) stop me from jumping into that pool, anyway. It felt wonderful until I nearly drowned—in the shallow end. That's when it dawned on me that perhaps swim lessons would be a nice way to work out. But of course I never got around to that, either, because ladies, you know the trials and tribulations of water and a black woman's hair—the shit don't mix.

The next time around, "Buns of Steel" was the goal, and the fact that this one could be done in the comfort of home, at my own pace, made me feel great. I threw on a pair of cross-trainers, some spandex shorts, and an exercise bra, and was ready to work it out. But no one had explained that to get buns of steel, you must first endure buns of pain. After five solid squats my buns were burning so bad, there was no need to go any further. With no one around to impress, I squatted on the sofa and watched the entire workout. Tired and hungry after all that talk about buns, I headed over to the mall and picked up one of those Cinnabon cinnamon rolls with extra icing. Walking the mall, I reasoned, was my workout for the day. And as over Billy Blanks as I was, the drama continued when a family friend who heard about my mission to get in shape gave me the entire Tae-Bo collection for Christmas. I politely said thank you and taped a fabulous low-cal cooking show over them. Before long workout videos were being tossed into the garage along with all the other mangled machines that had failed to give me results. And results were needed, because the NAACP Image Awards was approaching (I'd received my first nomination for Outstanding Actress in a Comedy Series for *The Parkers*), so you know a sister had to look good. In a fit of frustration, girlfriends encouraged me to fall in line, jump on the bandwagon, and call the man they called whenever they needed to get in shape quick.

So, I did the L.A. thing and hired a personal trainer. Now, y'all know I must have lost my mind if I agreed to pay someone to show up at my doorstep before the crack of dawn, wake me from my beauty sleep, and place me on a strict diet. But Keith was there like clockwork four days a week. It seemed like he got a thrill out of inflicting punishment. An ex-marine, Keith was in his forties but didn't look a day over twenty-five. He'd fought in Operation Desert Storm, and he seemed a little on the crazy side; every now and then he'd call me by my last name, tell me to drop and give him twenty-five, and scold me if I couldn't get through a strenuous series of stretches. And he wasn't taking the fact that I was a FATTY girl as an excuse. "Fat is no reason not to be fit," he barked. Once, during a set of push-ups, my arms became like noodles and were about to give out, but Keith was in my face, challenging me to suck it up and let the burn of the exercise do its thing. Another time, he had me jog a steep hill and halfway up barked, "Here you go, carry these." *These* was a pair of five-pound hand weights, in addition to the ankle weights and insulated workout suit I was already wearing. This punishment went on for about three weeks, but the straw that broke the camel's back was when this maniac told me to open my refrigerator. "What?" I said. "Open it," he barked. "This is an inspection." I proceeded to open the refrigerator and watched as this man tossed out a brand-new gallon of Häagen-Dazs butter pecan ice cream, a frozen Sara Lee cheesecake, and a roll of Pillsbury cookie mix. Then he headed to the pantry and got rid of a family-size bag of Nacho Cheese Doritos (damn, I love Doritos), a whole chocolate cake, and a carton of Ding-Dongs. And he wasn't done yet. Somehow Keith sniffed out two Krispy Kreme doughnuts I'd stashed in the sofa, pulled them from between the cushions, and uncovered another reserve hidden in the bushes out back. After the cupboards were bare, he then proceeded to school me on the pitfalls of unhealthy eating. Now, y'all know me, ordinarily I'd have something to say, but he was on his way out the door, so I let him rant and rave, anything just to get him to go. Then, as if this food fiasco never occurred, this psycho smiled and announced, "I'll see you at 0600 hours. Have a good day." All I could muster was a weak "Sir, yes, sir." I closed the door and knew it was the last time Keith would ever see me. I was so tired, I fell asleep right at the front door and stayed in that exact spot until he knocked the next morning. Instead of opening the door, I crawled over to my purse, wrote Sergeant Crazy a note that said leave me the hell alone, and slid it under the door. And when I got the strength, I climbed into the car and headed to the grocery store to replace all the goodies he threw away. That's when I decided the gym might not be such a bad place after all.

See, y'all, I've never liked gyms because most folks aren't there to get in shape. They're there to get their macks on, or to show off. And I'm not just talking about the men. Women have lost their minds, too. I've seen some so pumped up, I didn't know whether they were men or women. Then there are the helpless ones who use the gym as an excuse to get their flirt on, and chances are, they've all got one thing in common—they're evil and skinny. The thought of enduring another class, or walking by women who need to do a workout session at a Hometown Buffet, was enough to send me packing. But I was determined to tone this temple, come hell or high water, and that meant forgetting about the people and committing to the process. So, with less than a month before the BIG show, I rushed out and joined the premier fitness center in town. This one—like most in L.A.—wasn't your run-of-the-mill workout spot. It was a state-of-the-art facility that offered certified personal trainers, on-the-spot fitness evaluations, food consultants, and on-duty doctors at your beck and call around the clock. It also boasted a celebrity clientele, which meant the level of bullshit going on was far greater than at your typical gym. I don't know about y'all, but in Baltimore we just go to the gym and do our thing, but not in L.A. On the first day, I pulled up to the place and handed my keys to a well-dressed attendant who valet-parked my car. Then I entered this high-priced joint and was greeted by a life-size Ken doll, who was eager to sign me up. He began by explaining the current new-member specials, then offered to take me on a tour. This place was three stories and boasted an atrium, a gourmet restaurant, a whirlpool, sauna, masseuse, and nothing but twigs casing the joint. Shit, the tour alone was enough of a workout for one day, but Ken was just getting started. He performed a routine health evaluation, explained the benefits of good cardiovascular workouts, suggested a diet plan, and offered brochures that listed the gym's endless classes and services. I took one look at the schedule and knew Hip-Hop Dance Moves and Mountain Climbing 101 weren't gonna work for me. That's for those young, crazy, thin ones. Where's the Electric Slide class, or Slow Impact 101? I thanked him for the information and was done for the day, but before I could get the hell out of there, Ken suggested I check out a class starting in ten minutes.

When I entered the class, it was a slew of thin ones stretching and chatting amongst themselves. I attempted to speak, but it was obvious a F.A.T. girl wasn't going to be able to join the conversation, so I turned to an eighty-year-old woman who didn't have an ounce of body fat. She did, however, have a scowl on her face that let me know she was already in the zone. All of the sticks were color coordinated and dressed in the latest cute workout gear, while I had run out of the house in the F.A.T. girl workout uniform—the first BIG T-shirt available and a pair of biker shorts. When the instructor entered, I swear girlfriend was straight out of *Flashdance*. She had on a faceful of makeup, a hot pink leotard, a pair of pink leg warmers, and her name was Barbie. I knew I wasn't going to like her. She acknowledged her cohorts, then wasted no time getting into position. "All right ladies, grab your step boxes and let's get going," she chirped. They all nodded, applauded, and screamed their approval. Barbie put on a high-speed party CD, adjusted her headset, and took off like the Energizer Bunny. Her ass just kept going, and going, and going. Everyone was following right along, stepping up and down on their little boxes, throwing their hands in the air, and following along as Barbie screamed, "Ten, nine, eight, seven, six more, five, four more, three, two. Okay, now, eight more, seven, six." Clearly, Barbie had a problem counting, because after five minutes her ass was still screaming, "and five, four, three." She could never quite make it to one. Fifteen minutes felt like an hour as I stepped my size elevens on that little step box and pulled a muscle in my leg that I never even knew existed. I went down hard, too, y'all. I was dying, but Barbie and her stick clique just glanced my way, saw I wasn't dead, and never missed a beat. "Move to the side," Barbie announced as I attempted to get up and step around eighty-year-old Wonder Woman, who was still dry as a bone. Barbie didn't even attempt to help a newcomer out. It was just step at your own risk. That's right. Don't mess with skinny evil ones when they're getting a workout on. Damn it, we can't all jump around, so it would be nice to see instructors that wear more than a size four and don't move faster than the speed limit teaching classes. Shit, they can already raise their tree limbs over their heads, what about those of us that can't? There's no stomach to get in their way, what are those of us with tummies supposed to do? Skinny folks don't have to work hard to step-kick for thirty minutes. Damn it, we do. That was it. I hobbled my paralyzed self out of that class and took to the bed for the rest of the day. Of course, that was after stopping by the Popeye's drive-through for a three-piece snack. I would've gotten the usual six-piece, but hey, it was the first day of my workout regime, and I didn't want to overdo it. A few days later, after the muscles were back to normal, I decided to tackle a spin class. Now, riding a stationary bike can't be that hard, right? Maybe not in Milwaukee, but in L.A., instructors will have your ass riding up imaginary hills, standing up on bicycles for five minutes while pedaling, and performing arm extensions. On this day, the instructor was a young white guy named Gary, who seemed cool and understanding. Sensing my apprehension, Gary walked over, helped me get adjusted on the bicycle, and told me not to kill myself, just go at a nice even pace, and if anything started to hurt, just let him know. I said, "Thank you, baby. I will." I was feeling good about this session until Gary mounted his bike, pushed a button on the CD player, and took off like it was the Tour de France. Gary was one of those philosophical spinners who offered witty words with his workout. "Don't worry about where we're going or where we've been. Just stay in the moment," he urged. Clearly, I missed the meaning, but everyone else seemed to get it right away, because all of a sudden they started pedaling faster. Moments later Gary offered another pearl: "We can do this, one pedal stroke at a time." "That's right," shouted a PLUMP woman in the back. She kept pedaling along as the crowd screamed and biked faster, buying into the Gary credo. Ten minutes into this bike tour, I was over it and Gary. He was nice but started to get on my nerves with his pedaling up hills that didn't exist. Finally he urged us to "get out of our comfort zone and go someplace new." That's when I decided to follow Gary's sage advice. I got off that bicycle (mind you, it took a good ten minutes just to get one foot out of those damn stirrups), got into the car, and went to the new Roscoe's House of Chicken & Waffles right down the street. Even though the culprit wasn't a skinny evil one this time, the entire gym experience just didn't suit me. BIG girls, perhaps that's been your experience, too. There's something about gyms that ain't right—like no F.A.T. instructors.

That's why I propose, the next time you decide to get your workout on, ladies, just show up with a group of your F.A.T. friends and dominate the entire class. So what if you can't keep up? Go anyway, and slow the whole damn thing down. Hell, we've got to stay in shape, too, and it's time the enemy deals with us on their stomping ground. Though there's no law that says achieving that goal has to happen in a hot-ass gym. Jogging from the dinner table to the sofa is exercise. Sweating over a marvelous four-course meal, now that's a serious workout, and getting the heart rate pumping by lugging in bags of your favorite snacks from the grocery store has surely got to count for something. BIG girls, don't let sticks pressure you into doing things at top speed. Shit, we're FLUFFY, which means we've got to do things the FLUFFY way—slowly. I lasted at that gym for about a week before I said "Later" to the whole ugly experience. But I was still determined. I thought perhaps a totally new approach was necessary.

My sister-in-law had been reading countless books on weight lifting and power eating, and somehow I let her talk me into joining her as she did the diet thing. Now, there are countless weight-loss plans out there that promise amazing results, and Lord knows, we did them all. First it was the no-carb diet. (That one only lasted from breakfast to lunch; when she told me no carbs meant no rice, no potatoes, no pasta, and no bread and butter, I told her, uh, NO DAMN WAY.) Then there was the seven-day cabbage diet (if I never see another cabbage again, it'll be too soon); the high-protein diet (loved this one. Especially since I could eat all the steak, chicken, and bacon I wanted—and did); the eat-right-for-your-blood-type diet (which might've worked if I knew my blood type); and finally the Hollywood 48-Hour Miracle Diet. Shit, the only miracle was that I didn't pass out from this two-day juice fast that promised to burn body fat and have you lose up to ten pounds in the first two days. It worked. I lost seven pounds, but damn if I didn't gain ten back the moment I returned to solid foods. But none of these ridiculous take-the-weight-off quick plans compares to the Zone diet. Baby, this one was crazy. For seven weeks you must commit to eating a precise 40/30/30 carbohydrate/protein/fat ratio of foods prepared by award-winning chefs. At a price tag of more than $1,000 a month, folks from Zone Gourmet deliver three freshly prepared meals and two snacks to your doorstep in an insulated bag, all by 6:00 A.M. daily. Is that some L.A. shit, or what? I was hesitant at first because for that much money, I like my bags to say Popeye's, Red Lobster, or Ruth Chris Steak House on the side, but what the hell. I was in it to win it. The first morning my little insulated bag arrived, I picked it up off the porch, and the shit was so light, I thought it was empty. When I finally unzipped it and took a look, it was six small containers. I thought to myself, Did I just get played? I could've eaten the entire day's supply of food in just one sitting. One container labeled "breakfast" held scrambled egg whites, fruited oatmeal, and four nuts. The snack container held one Ritz cracker with a square of cheese and a teaspoon of peanut butter. I kid you not. And I was mad, because it was a Ritz, and you can't eat just one of those. And dinner was chicken lentil stew. What the hell is a lentil, anyway? My sister-in-law called to ask how breakfast was. "Terrible," I told her. "I swear if I didn't have an audition to rush off to, I would've been in the kitchen frying up a couple pieces of bacon to go along with those egg whites, fruited oatmeal, and four nuts." She couldn't wait to share the fact that she was full from her scrambled egg whites, fruited oatmeal, and four nuts. By the time I arrived at that audition, I was in the zone, all right—the hungry zone. I was light-headed, talking incoherently, and stumbling. Folks thought I was on drugs and started to whisper, point, and stare. I wanted to scream, I'm not on drugs, I'm on the Zone, but I was too damn weak to form a sentence. That's when I remembered an old candy bar in my purse. I pulled that little Butterfinger out and ate it like it was a T-bone steak. But the sugar rush threw me out of the zone, by the time the casting director called me in, I was so damn delirious, instead of reading my role, I read every damn word on the page, without stopping, including the casting director's role and the stage directions, too. I was so hungry after I left that audition, I headed straight to the nearest Popeye's drive-through, ordered a two-piece wing basket, took it home, and ate it right along with my Zone Chicken Lentil Stew. Don't laugh. I paid a lot of money for that Zone food, and I'll be damned if I was gonna let it go to waste. I couldn't stay in the zone seven hours, much less seven weeks.

When fad diets failed, it was on to diet centers like Weight Watchers, which has helped millions of people around the world lose weight. The company's signature Winning Points System allows you to eat the foods you want and still lose weight. And the best part of all, no food is off limits. You can eat any of your favorites, including fast food and sweets, and still see success on the scale. This sounded like the program for me. But when the diet counselors started explaining how foods are based on regular serving sizes and how "eyeballing" servings lets you know how much to eat, I knew right away it wasn't going to work. The problem with the Winning Points

System? BIG eaters can't win. Because when I see good food, trust me, my eyes are always BIGGER than my stomach, especially if it's butter pecan ice cream, one of my mama's sweet potato pies, or some garlic mashed potatoes. I gave it a try, but all the good stuff cost too many damn points. One scoop of ice cream was four points, a slice of pizza was nine points, and a bottle of beer cost three points. Shit, trying to find the right mix of carbs and protein to keep me satisfied was too damn difficult, and after a while, rather than count points, I just started counting pieces of food instead. Math was never a strong subject in school, and WW's points system was too damn complicated, so three pieces of pizza became three points, and one scoop of ice cream, one point. The only thing that lost weight was my wallet.

Next, I tried Jenny Craig. Jenny promised a whole new life and individualized support from consultants who would work with me every step of the way. But my schedule is hectic, and sitting down and talking to a counselor every day gets to be a bit ridiculous. Especially when the counselor is a former JC convert (and a fan of the show), who wants to spend hours extolling the virtues of the program, and calls to scold me if I forget to check in. I was about done with the crazy weight-loss centers until a very dear friend suggested Lindora's Lean for Life Program. After dropping thirty-five pounds—and enduring months of five A.M. workouts, treadmill runs, and a low-carb diet—girlfriend looked great. But in no time she went from a JOLLY one of us to a member of the E-Team, and she was so thrilled with her new little self that whenever someone complimented her, the first thing out of girlfriend's mouth was, "It's a size four, wanna see the label?" No, I don't want to see the label. I want to see you pick up a piece of fried catfish and a couple of hush puppies. Lindora worked for her, but I decided to check out something a little less strenuous.

Like yoga. BIG girls, this is one exercise where we don't have to jump around, worry about breaking machines, or stumble out of the door paralyzed. The art of yoga involves a nice, peaceful series of movements that require you to hold positions for an extended period of time. That doesn't mean you don't get a workout. Yoga is a total fitness program with results like an optimum physique, high levels of concentration, and boundless energy. But its goals extend beyond the physical. It challenges and perfects the body. Postures like the Full Boat pose and the Upward-Facing Dog had me bedridden, but that wasn't a problem, because when my husband got home, I used a few of those new yoga moves on him and got the best workout of all. Note to the CHUNKY and FUNKY: Throw the Half Tortoise pose, the Camel pose, or my all-time favorite, the Dead Body pose—where you simply lie flat on your back—and you can get your workout, rest, and freak on simultaneously. Lovemaking can burn those extra calories you piled on during that romantic dinner, and stretch and tone just about every muscle in the body. It's much more enjoyable than swimming twenty laps, and baby, you don't even need special sneakers to do it.

Speaking of special—it's hard not to mix with skinny folks in the Valley of the Dolls, and though most tend to act crazy, I've crossed paths with a few cool thin ones. One sister in particular was a dancer. Girlfriend and I hit it off right away because she always greeted me with a smile, complimented me, and made me feel special. Though she weighed about eighty pounds, this sister never tried to convince me to lose weight—though I tried to FATTEN her up a few times. One night, we got to talking and sharing our concerns about

WEIGHTY issues. She wanted to gain weight, and I told her about my frustration of trying to get toned when you're BIG-boned and the aggravation of having to bend, stretch, and kick when you've got extra POUNDAGE to consider, and how I wanted to develop a workout for BIG girls. Because ladies, it's time we had a workout of our own, led by a BIG girl, that offers a series of nice, easy steps that won't leave us winded and in need of an ambulance. She offered to choreograph it and called a few weeks later to say she had videotaped a little something she wanted to show me. When she popped that tape in, it started off cool, but then girlfriend must have forgotten her target audience, because it turned into a routine for B2K, or one of those other fast-moving little boy bands. Halfway through, she broke out with a series of kicks and lunges that belonged in the Ringling Brothers and Barnum and Bailey circus—and there were way too many of them. And she seemed to have the same counting problem as Barbie, because her skinny ass could never quite make it to one. I asked, "Girl, that was great, but, uh, who the hell is supposed to do those acrobatics?" Usher? There's no way me or any other BIG girl is doing fifty of anything. Shit, this is called the BIG-GIRL WORKOUT. Our moves need to come in twos—like two squats, two leg lifts, two arm extensions, and in between each of those combinations needs to be two minutes of rest. And if you really want us to get excited, make the damn tape ten minutes long, because after that, we lose interest. Shit, after five minutes, I'm already thinking about whether the exercise reward should be a doughnut or a scoop of Ben & Jerry's Chunky Monkey. And forget moving swiftly, because we're doing it at whatever pace feels comfortable that day. See, ladies, that's the difference between the BIG and small—speed and exercise choices. Extending that arm to pick up a piece of chicken is just as good an exercise as an empty arm extension. And if it needs to be higher impact and more weight, just extend that arm with a couple of chicken breasts rather than a wing and do it at a faster pace. Even our choice of beverage is different. While the tiny are guzzling gallons of designer water, we like to quench our thirst with a sip of Coca-Cola because you need something refreshing—and strong—to keep the sugar level up when moving at warp speed.

But I've got a bone to pick with some of the TUBBY troops. Word has gotten out that some of y'all are acting up. That's right. Friendships are falling apart, and the culprit is weight, or should I say, loss of it. I've gotten letters, and significant weight loss is pitting BIG girls against each other, like two stressed-out sisters—a sexy sixteen and a terrific twenty— down in Birmingham. Now, despite the fact that these two had been childhood buddies, had great jobs, and had family and friends who loved them, both shared a desire to lose weight, and they decided the only way to do it was together. For months they walked after work, took the stairs, and tried to watch what they ate, but none of that gave them the results they desired. So Miss Sixteen talked her girl into the two-for-one special at the gym, and that's when all hell broke loose. After a routine evaluation to determine each lady's fitness level, the smaller of the two was giddy over the fact that she was able to do twenty leg lifts while her girl could barely get to five. After a couple months, Miss Sixteen had moved on to one-hour spin classes, mastered the Tae-Bo workout, and was training for a triathlon. Her girl, disappointed that she wasn't able to lose weight faster, gave up. After a while, whenever Miss Twenty called to check in, she noticed she couldn't even get a return phone call. Suddenly her girl had a new crew and wasn't interested in their Sunday all-you-can-eat ritual. The former Miss Sixteen had dwindled down to a size eight and had turned into the worst kind of eight—an evil one. She shunned Lane Bryant and was so busy squeezing her new figure into chic threads from Ann Taylor, Express, and Banana Republic that she didn't have time to check on her friend. But that's the way it goes when some FAT folks get in shape—they get all "new" and act as if they don't know you anymore. Sure, girlfriend worked hard to slim down, and goodie for her, but damn it, what about us? Why do you have to leave FATTY girls behind who were there when you were getting your chow on right along with us? Instead of encouraging her friend, this one couldn't wait to join the enemy. I'm telling you, ladies, the gym is the enemy, and if you don't believe that losing weight makes folks crazy, then what the hell is wrong with Richard Simmons? Is it me, or does Richard seem out of sorts, like since he lost all that damn weight he doesn't quite know what to do with himself, or that he should put on more than those damn little shorts? I swear Richard looks like all he needs to get back on track is a good prime rib dinner. But you can skip meals, work out seven days a week, spend thousands, and still end up crazy; I know, because it happened to me.

After killing myself to look good, I woke up one day and said, NO MORE. Well, let me keep it real. It was a few days before the announcement of nominees, and I was starting to see shit that wasn't really there. I called my brother, Steve, and told him I had to get somewhere quick because I was starting to lose it. So I drove myself to a hospital and checked in. The doctor diagnosed my condition as exhaustion and sedated me. I was so messed up that when Steve got to the hospital, I told him to look how the money had messed me up. The doctor told him all I needed was a few days' rest. That night I slept like a baby. But the next day, when Steve came by to visit, he reminded me that the NAACP Image Awards announcements were the next day. I said, Well, damn it, what are we waiting for, let's get the hell out of here. As he was helping me out of bed, the doctor came in and asked where I was going. I told him that I had to leave because I was an NAACP IMAGE AWARD NOMINEE. Thinking I was still delusional, the doctor told me I wasn't ready to leave just yet and attempted to help me back into the bed. But I was adamant, and with Steve on one side trying to break me out of this crazy house, and the doctor trying to keep me in, I announced in my most dramatic voice, "You don't understand, Doctor, I am an NAACP Image Award nominee, and I must go." Assuming I was some half-crazy starlet trying to be difficult, he relented, told me if I cracked up, the hospital wasn't responsible, and made me sign a release form. I scribbled my name, grabbed my coat, and Steve and I were out the door. Now, the only reason this story is funny is because I really *was* an NAACP Image Award nominee. After one too many lose-weight-quick schemes, fatigue truly was the only thing wrong with me. However, had I not realized it, I might have lost the most important thing of all—my mind. That's the way it goes in Hollywood. Folks go through turmoil just to fit an image and refuse to reveal their real weight loss secret—plastic surgery. Yep, that's the real E(vil) True Hollywood Story, and that's where I draw the line. The only knife touching me will be the one in my hand cutting into a juicy piece of meat.

And the real meat of the matter is that it's difficult to achieve real weight loss with all of the conflicting messages. We don't know whether to eat carbs, limit carbs, make it a high-protein diet or a no-protein one. You can read labels and count carbs all day long and still not lose weight. And while I don't want to send the message that you have to lose weight to be beautiful, BIG girls, I do want to say that good health is imperative. It's no secret that diabetes, heart disease, stroke, and high blood pressure all work against us when we're heavy, so take good care of yourself, see a doctor regularly, and if the gym isn't for you, find something that is. It's a proven fact that staying in shape is the key to a healthy life. And if that's what it takes to keep your loveliness lovely, then do it somehow, some way. But damn it, don't hurt yourself like I did. After yo-yo diets, inferior gym equipment, and crazed workouts, I've decided to commit to a healthier lifestyle that includes moderate exercise (done the BIG-girl way—slowly) and a balanced diet (that *does* include some carbs). Once my obsession for perfection passed, it was as if The Man Upstairs said, Thank you, my child, for finally realizing that I didn't place you in this crazy town to resemble everyone else. I brought you here to represent for the FULL-SIZE flock. From then on, my Hollywood goals changed. After zoning out at auditions, my mission became to fatten up a few folks in Hollywood. I started showing up with plates of chocolate chip cookies, sock-it-to-me cakes, and my famous honey-dipped fried chicken, and when I checked in, casting directors got my name and a basket of gourmet goodies. Did it work, you ask? Trust me, as stressed out as some of those casting directors are, it was welcomed with a smile, and if you caught me in the films *Baby Boy*, *Three Strikes*, and *Two Can Play That Game*, then you know it worked like a charm. They may not have initially thought to go Fabulous and Thick, but by the time I left, they were damn sure thinking (as they were chewing), maybe a F.A.T. girl wouldn't be such a bad idea after all.

Oh, and if you're wondering how the NAACP Image Awards turned out. I won. And that night was one of the

proudest of my life. Wearing a sequined, form-fitting, one-shoulder jersey knit dress with a keyhole center to show off my captivating cleavage, I marched up on that stage and accepted that award for every F.A.T. girl who was told she would never make it. And ladies, I was exactly the size I wanted to be—a tantalizing twenty-two. That's right, I was still the same little girl from Baltimore whose daddy called her the prettiest thing in the world. But this time, with a renewed sense of self and an understanding that Hollywood doesn't need another starved starlet, I stepped past the sticks, representing the dawn of a new day in H-Town.

F.A.T. Girls' Survival Tips:

WHILE EXERCISING—

* Show up with a crew of F.A.T. friends and slow down the class.

* For energy, drink Coke, not water.

* If it starts to burn, stop.

SEVEN

Travel—but Not If You're Big

PLANES, TRAINS, AUTOMOBILES

I LOVE TO TRAVEL. Meeting my fans up close and personal is what makes all of this madness so memorable. But getting to the people can be hell; especially since the travel industry doesn't make it easy—or comfortable—for us. I guess they figure PUDGY passengers aren't interested in seeing Paris in the spring, flying off to London in the fall, or laying our BIG asses on sandy beaches in the Caribbean during the summer. As far as they're concerned, we should just pitch a tent in the back-yard or flip on the Travel Channel. But I'm not about to just sit at home because I'm LARGE and lovely. My F.A.T. friends and I want to travel and see the world, too. So make way, because whether by plane, train, or automobile, we're coming.

Before the television shows came along, stand-up was my livelihood, and to this day, I still travel on weekends to perform somewhere. But like so many things, the events of

September 11, 2001, have made travel—and life—much more
difficult. However, I refuse to let the craziness (or a bunch of
crazy fanatics) keep me from my fans. God is my copilot, and
wherever he leads, I will go. I just wish he wasn't leading me to
airports all the time. The airlines aren't a BIG person's best
friend—in fact, they treat us more like the enemy. The first
hurdle is getting through security. By the time I've hauled it
from the curb, I'm breathless, and the last thing I, or any
F.A.T. person, wants to hear is that our luggage is too BIG to
fit through that tiny X-ray machine. And they look at you like,
Sorry, it isn't going. Oh, yes, it is. I'm not leaving without my
valuables, which means if I've got to roll up my sleeves, take
matters into my own hands, and shove my BIG bag through,
and then try to get through myself, it's going. Then it's
"Excuse me, ma'am, but can you please open your bag?" And
that's fine. I'm happy to oblige, but don't inspect my gear and
then tell me it's too heavy to make the flight. Take a look at
me. Of course my luggage is HEAVY. I'm HEAVY. Which
means I can't just throw a few little things into the suitcase.
I've got to roll my BIG purses, pants, shoes, and of course a
few snacks in, and position them just right. And speaking of
right, I believe the right thing for the airlines to do is to find a
way to accommodate TUBBY travelers, but they're too busy
trying to make up for the billions they're losing in revenue—
and packing us in like sardines—to figure out a better solution. Once we do finally fight security, wrestle to make it onto
the airplane, and find our stretcher of a seat, a BIG person's
best bet is to stay put, because any extra movement could be
life-threatening, or at best dangerous—like going to the rest
room. Once you shimmy out of the seat, make it down that
narrow aisle without knocking anyone in the head with your
hips, and wait ten minutes to use the tiny toilet, the plane is

making its initial descent. And you definitely don't want to get stuck in the can. But hey, that's the chance you take. If you don't pee on yourself trying to get into that tight little space, then hold on, because you'll pee everywhere but into the toilet—that is, if you can find it. And good luck trying to get to the toilet paper—or getting it off your pumps—because bending down is a bitch, and turning around in that claustrophobic box is definitely out of the question. I got stuck in one once and panicked so bad, I broke out in hives. So, LARGE ladies and gents, you know what that means. There'll be no Mile High Club for us. In case you aren't aware, that's the unofficial club where you experience the thrill of getting your "freak" on from 35,000 feet in an airplane bathroom. You can try it if you want to, but fuck around and get stuck and they'll be coming to dislodge you from that little nook, and an armed officer will be hauling you away the moment the plane lands. That's why I say if you're F.A.T., just join the Mile High Club right in your seat. But don't expect that little-ass blanket to cover you up, or to find a flight attendant to bring you one.

Whatever happened to the good old days when flight attendants served you with a smile? There should be some regulation that says after they reach a certain age, they should have to hang up their wings. Some of them are old—and evil as hell. I learned that on a carrier whose slogan used to be "Fly the friendly skies." Hell, there wasn't nothin' friendly about this airline or its funky flight attendants. I was headed to Chicago, and the plane was freezing. Good thing I had my BLUBBER blanket to keep me warm, because when I rang the call buzzer to request a blanket, no one responded. So I waited a few moments and rang it again. Still no one. Finally, I turned around (there was no way I was getting up from that stretcher) and summoned a flight attendant who was a couple of aisles away. I swear it took five minutes for her to mosey down the aisle, and when she finally got there, she'd run out of blankets and handed me a pillow instead. I already had a pillow and told her it was a blanket I wanted. Girlfriend snatched the pillow back with her old shriveled-up hand and drifted up the aisle in a huff. After trying to stay warm (and requesting a blanket five more times—girlfriend's Alzheimer's was clearly in full effect), I finally got the last one on the airplane. But when I went to unfold it, I swear, the shit only covered one thigh. I fought all night long for a dinner napkin. What I want to know is, where are the blankets for the FULL-FIGURED, full-fare-paying passengers? After spending thousands for a seat, it doesn't make sense that we should have to freeze. That's why, now, I travel with my own cover—and my own stash of food, because I'll be damned if I'm going to freeze and starve to death, too. And trust me, they will starve you.

I'm telling you, flying is an entirely different thing than in the old days when folks dressed up and flight attendants were nice. Today, you're lucky if they even crack a smile. That's really a shame; if they aren't going to make airplanes comfortable and the flight attendants friendly, the least they could do is make the food tasty—that is, if they feed us at all. Today, they just throw a bag or two of peanuts our way and keep it movin' like we're a bunch of circus animals. How is anyone—except a skinny bitch—supposed to make it on a six-hour flight from Los Angeles to New York on two packs of peanuts and a Coke? And is there some law that says airlines are required to pass out the saltiest damn nuts and pretzels they can find? After a couple of those, your mouth is as dry as the Mojave Desert, but don't you dare ask for the entire can of Coke to wash it down. Those evil ones will look at you like you stole something. Once, I was headed down to Atlanta for a Queens of Comedy performance and had rushed from the TV set to the airport with no time to eat. I was so hungry I couldn't see straight. When I finally made it on the airplane, I was ready for those salty peanuts, but you aren't going to believe this one. There was a passenger on board who was violently allergic to peanuts, and even the smell of peanut oil made her ill. She alerted the flight attendants, and a few moments later the captain came over the loudspeaker and announced that because there was a passenger on board allergic to peanuts, no one could have any. So, the other 150 passengers on the airplane had to just starve because of one woman. And this skinny bitch had the nerve to pull out a salad she'd bought in the terminal and proceed to chow down. I should have told them I was allergic to the smell of lettuce. Let her skinny ass starve, too. And the airlines think they're slick. They knew this woman couldn't have peanuts before they closed the doors and took off, but they didn't let us know about it until we were in the air so they could still keep all the revenue. As hungry as I was, I would've taken the next flight. Shit, I'll get off the plane if I can't have something to eat. Instead, I just closed my eyes and tried not to let the hunger headache overpower me. The moment we landed, I stepped off that plane and immediately knew there was a God. Baby, staring me right in the face was a Popeye's Fried Chicken. I don't care if it was six o'clock in the morning, I stepped up to the counter, and the folks could see I was having Popeye withdrawals. They were just gearing up for the day, and shit wasn't quite ready, but I promised tickets to the show to the first person who could produce a biscuit, a wing, something. They hooked me up with a couple of biscuits and honey, and a couple of wings from the back. That little snack set me straight until I could get to the hotel for a real breakfast. See, that's why Atlanta's Hartsfield International Airport gets an A-plus in my book. They give F.A.T. folks exactly what we want— good food. And, they put it within reach.

But I can't say the same for the Chicago O'Hare and Dallas/Fort Worth airports. Oh, I love the people in Chi-town, and my friends down in the Big D are the best, but baby, those are the two worst, most confusing airports in the country, especially if you're carrying a few extra pounds. Shit, even skinny folks get winded trying to make it from one gate to the next at DFW. Just once I'd like to land at Terminal A, Gate 1, and leave from Terminal A, Gate 3, but that never happens. The connecting gate is at least a mile away. It's probably another one of those cleverly disguised ploys of the airlines to generate additional revenue by making you miss your flight, so you'll have to buy a new ticket. It never fails. We arrive at Gate 1, Terminal A, and our connecting flight leaves from Gate 81, Terminal C—in forty-five minutes. Now, that leaves one of three ways to get to your connection. You can walk. But you'll be dead before you can even make it a quarter of a mile. You can take the tram, but trying to find the damn thing is another journey all its own—if you fuck around and miss your stop, guess what, you've missed your connecting flight, too. Or you can try to hail one of those carts that go whizzing by. And good luck getting it; they're never around when you need them, or the minute you do spot one and try to flag it down, guess who's taking up prime cart space—a crew of skinny folks, of course. Shit, sometimes I wanna knock someone in the head and tell 'em to move. Get out the way. And flagging down a ride is happening, of course, while you're trudging through the terminal because you've got to keep it moving, or you'll be moving into a nice comfortable chair for the evening because you missed the last flight. Before you know it, you've trekked ten miles, and there's not even one decent fast food joint on the journey. Shit, a pack of F.A.T. foxes trying to get through DFW will be a pack of evil skinny bitches by the time they make it to their final destination—the next gate.

And once you do make it to the Promised Land, just short of heart failure, you discover there's no boarding pass attached to your ticket, and the line is twenty-five deep. Here comes another fight, because you know what seat they're going to try to give you—32E, of course. There should be a law that if you weigh 200 pounds or more you must automatically be given an aisle or a window seat, not a freakin' middle. Trust me, in the long run it'll help ALL passengers—not just the F.A.T. ones. We desperately need aisles so we can get a little more personal space and not squeeze folks to death. But that doesn't stop money-hungry airlines from assigning our BIG asses a middle seat, without a seatbelt extension, leaving us stuffed in like sausages, anyway.

As frustrating as air travel has become, I'm surprised no one has come up with an airline exclusively for us. Call it F.A.T. Airways. I'm telling you, they'd make a fortune, because F.A.T. America (and there are a lot of us) is tired of the chaos associated with trying to fly. Seats are a problem. Food is a problem. The bathrooms are a problem. And, those evil flight attendants are definitely a BIG problem. On F.A.T. Airways, none of those things would be a concern. You wouldn't have to worry about the lack of space, or potentially spilling over into another person's seat, because the seats would be La-Z-Boy recliners with enough room that you don't have to worry about knocking out the passenger behind you. You can just lie back and get comfortable. If you meet someone on the airplane you think is fine, and you want to get to know each other a little better, there'll be lounges with plenty of room to go and talk, and maybe even for PLUMP people to do their thing, if you know what I mean, Mile High wannabes. That's right, there will finally be some MEGA Mile High Club members. And the aisles would be nice and WIDE, so you don't have to hit folks in the head just to get to the rest room. And the food, baby, it would be a buffet where you could come up and serve yourself as much as you want. The frequent-flier program would be based on meals eaten. And the flight attendants would be southern women with warm, charming personalities who anticipate your needs before you ever know you need anything. I'm telling you, our own airline is the answer, or at the very least, mandatory aisles for the MEATY. That simple law would alleviate all of the discomfort associated with airline travel, and perhaps all the lawsuits.

A few years ago there were a number of reports in the news about F.A.T. folks being forced to buy extra seats to accommodate their extra POUNDAGE. One lawsuit in particular was brought on by a businessman who claimed he was inconvenienced because he had to fly across the country sitting next to a FAT man. The thin man was upset because during the entire flight, the FAT man's BLUBBER kept spilling over into his seat. And, to make matters worse, Mr. BIG was stuffed into a middle seat and had an injured foot. Whenever the thin man needed to get up to go to the rest room, Mr. BIG asked that he just step over him because it was too painful to move. Mr. BIG also had a problem putting his tray down because his belly got in the way, so he asked the thin man if he would mind if he put his drink on his tray. Now, I'd be mad, too, if a complete stranger asked to invade my personal space for six hours. It's horrible that the thin man was subjected to such discomfort and felt it necessary to bring about a lawsuit.

Clearly something needed to be done. But what solution did the airlines come up with? Their bright idea was to make F.A.T. folks buy an extra seat. Now, come on, y'all. That shit is flat-out discrimination. We are guests on your airline. Our comfort should be your primary concern. Hell, if it weren't for your frequent fliers, where would you be? Probably out of business, like TWA, Eastern, and Pan Am. And the way some of you act, it won't be long. I followed the case closely. Mr. BIG just happened to be a two-million-mile-a-year flier, but that didn't matter one bit. After that trip, the carrier sent a letter stating that if he planned to travel with them in the future, he'd be required to buy an extra seat. Did it really have to come to that? Surely there could have been a more equitable solution to the FAT-versus-skinny matter, a more customer-friendly way to make all parties happy.

You bet there was, and the better carrier found it. American Airlines calls itself "something special in the air." Instead of getting caught up in the FAT-fray, American was the first airline to remove extra seats from their entire fleet, giving fliers—BIG and small—more room throughout coach to spread out. Free at last, free at last, thank God Almighty, the F.A.T. are free at last—well, on AA, anyway. But it's a start. I'm sure that while the other carrier was sending a letter telling Mr. BIG he'd have to buy two seats, American was sending a welcome letter to join their frequent-flier program and transferring all two million of his miles—and the revenue he generated, too. See, that's what I'm talking about. Damn it, we may be F.A.T., but we've got rights, too. And we're going to exercise them. If you're going to charge us for an extra seat, then damn it, give us our extra frequent-flier miles and extra meals, too. So what if it tastes like cardboard? We paid for it, we want it. We also want some damn respect. Don't humiliate us in front of the entire airplane, like one airline did when my brother and I were on our way to the Caribbean. We were minding our own business when a flight attendant came by and informed me that the other F.A.T. passenger and I couldn't sit on the same side of the airplane. They called it a matter of weight and balance. Now, they saw us when we checked in, so why did they wait until we were settled in to inform us that we're both too damn BIG to sit on the same side? We moved, and though I was a little pissed about it, I decided not to let this ruin our trip. But wouldn't you know it, by the time we finally got buckled in and I closed my eyes, a skinny little flight attendant was banging her way up the aisle with one of those heavy carts. When she nearly took my shoulder out, I wanted to scream, That's the weight that's throwing off the balance of the plane, you crazy woman! No wonder folks are losing their cool in the air. If you were stuffed in like a sausage for six hours, you'd probably go a little stir-crazy too.

Sometimes, I feel like a crazy woman, on the road more than twenty-five weeks a year. That's why you better be careful what you ask for, because you just may get it. I prayed for this, so you won't hear me complain. But there have been times when I've gotten off one plane, and Steve has been at the gate with another suitcase full of fresh clothes for me to take another flight out of town. Like they did to a lot of folks, the terrorist attacks left me more than a bit shaken. I even considered staying on the ground for a while—that is, until I got an offer I couldn't refuse. In no time I was headed back to the not-so-friendly skies and to the scene of one of the most horrific crimes this country has ever faced—I was going to New York.

Last year, when legendary TV/film producer Suzanne

DePasse took over as the executive producer of *Showtime at the Apollo*, she called and asked if I would be the new host. Baby, what a thrill. Like a lot of folks, my career began on the Apollo stage, and to be asked to return as host was more than an honor, it was a dream come true. But that meant traveling between Los Angeles, where we shoot *The Parkers*, and New York, where the Apollo is filmed. And I'm telling you, that L.A. to New York commute is no joke. After years of traveling coach, I knew that unless they were flying me in first class, it wasn't going to happen. And it was no problem. Suzanne and her folks were more than accommodating. They sent a car to pick me up, handled my bags with care, reserved a comfortable suite, and treated me like a true Queen of Comedy. It was none of the hustle that I usually encountered. Y'all, I was excited to finally get a chance to see what goes on when they close that little blue curtain that separates first class from coach, and baby, it's a different world in the front half of the airplane.

First of all, the service is impeccable. They didn't have La-Z-Boys, but you could definitely get lost in those BIG leather seats that recline like beds and feature footrests. And it's like a Blockbuster Video store up there, with individual movie screens and a menu of movie selections that are yours for the asking. The flight attendants are cool thin ones who address you by name and are ready, willing, and able to assist you with placing your belongings in the overhead bins. There are no napkin-size covers, just BIG fluffy blankets, as soft as bedspreads, that are in the seat before you board. One attendant—of the two assigned to me—asked what I wanted to drink before takeoff and returned with a Malibu and Coke and a dinner menu. A menu? Then, she was back with warm, salted nuts, the good mix of cashews, almonds, peanuts, and walnuts, served in fine china, and another fresh drink. Before I could settle in, she returned with a pad to take my order. "The filet mignon," I said. "Sure, Ms. Mo'Nique. Anything else?" I thought she was joking. Shit, I've seen the portions on planes, and that was a loaded question. "Pardon me?" I said, not sure I heard her right. "Would you like a second entrée to go along with the steak?" "Why, yes," I chuckled. "I was just trying to decide between the shrimp and the chicken. Ah what the hell, give me the shrimp and the chicken, too," I tested, knowing that request would be impossible. "No problem." She smiled. "Coming right up." I thought to myself, damn, is this legal? Apparently it was, because after the nuts, a salad arrived; after the salad, it was appetizer crab legs (and I'm from Baltimore, so you know I was in heaven); and after the crab, the steak, chicken, and shrimp trio arrived, accompanied by a generous helping of mashed potatoes and grilled asparagus. And the shit was tasty, too. But nothing could top the hot fudge sundae and freshly baked chocolate chip cookies waiting in the wings. Now, you know I love to eat, but even I was full—so full I said no thank you to the cookies (there was no way I was passing up that hot fudge sundae, though). The flight attendant looked at me like I was crazy. "Oh, you must have just one cookie," she insisted. "No, thank you," I said again. But she wouldn't take no for an answer. "I'll just wrap some up for you to go," she asserted. "Fine," I said. Stuffed like a turkey, all I wanted to do was drift off, but they kept checking in to ensure that everything was okay. I swear, up front, the only thing you have to ask for is to be left alone, and I was just tipsy enough to do it. After three good hours of sleep, Miss Perky was back up again, this time with a morning breakfast tray of fruit and zucchini bread. By the time we landed at JFK, I was refreshed and ready to go. I tell you, like my daddy told me, it cost a little bit more to go first class, but damn it, that's the only place I want to be. There's nothing like flying in comfort, especially to tackle a city like New York.

Now, this wasn't my first trip to the BIG Apple, but it was the second time I was seeing it like a star. A driver was at the baggage claim area, holding a sign with my name on it, folks were at the gate waiting to help me with my bags, and everyone was making a fuss. When I arrived at the hotel, it wasn't a room, it was a luxurious suite. It all felt so great, but at the same time, so Hollywood. The first time I played the Apollo, I paid my own way, couldn't afford a hotel, and had to change clothes on 125th Street. And you want to know what I had on? I sported a BIG orange leather skirt suit with white opaque stockings and a pair of black patent leather pumps. Baby, you couldn't tell me nothing. I knew I was S-H-A-R-P. Looking back now, that shocking ensemble was definitely a fashion faux pas, but you've got to crawl before you can walk. Trust me, there's no orange this time, unless it's from my own collection. But with all the hoopla going on, I wanted a reality check. Folks who know me know I like to keep it real. Get out. Feel the city. And walk amongst the people. So Steve and I decided to take the train down to the Village.

We headed underground at the 125th Street station, and the minute we descended the stairway, I nearly fainted from the funk. But hey, it's New York, and we were keepin' it real, right? So, I didn't let a little funk fake me out. We were on an adventure. After a few minutes the train pulled up, the doors flew open, and we jumped on, but when I went to sit my F.A.T.ness down on one of those hard-ass seats, y'all, I nearly bounced off. Where's the cush? Good thing I've got it built in. No wonder New Yorkers wear a scowl; their booties hurt from having to sit on those hard-ass seats for hours. And when we got on, it was pretty empty, but as we made our way down-town, all of a sudden it became like a mini Apollo. Folks were singing, juggling shit, and selling toys, and not one person paid them any attention. One man was so bad, I wanted to jump up and Wop him like we do at the Apollo when an act stinks. Where is Omar (our Wop Wop man, who taps bad acts off the stage) when you need him? At one point, Steve and I thought we heard the conductor say Times Square, but the shit was so muffled and fast, who knew. So we jumped up. That's when an old lady jumped into my seat. It wasn't Times Square, but there's no going back in NYC. Move your meat, lose your seat. So I stood amongst this massive crowd. There's no such thing as personal space in a crowded city like New York; it's just get in where you fit in. For the first time, I knew how skinny folks on airplanes felt. People were leaning on me while reading the paper, and touching me in places only my man is allowed to go. At one point, I wanted to say back it up, but they have that glazed New York look like, deal with it, lady. I almost lost Steve in the crowd, until I looked around and spotted a glimpse of his bald head. But after about the fifth person stepped on my toe, and I spotted one of those underground Dunkin' Donuts, I signaled to him that it was time to bail out. After trying to maneuver through Times Square, I had had enough of keepin' it real. I needed to really get back to the hotel and soak my feet.

We decided to take a cab back, but getting around on top of the ground ain't so easy, either. I swear, hailing a cab in New York is a damn art form. Someone should tell folks that unless the medallion number on top of the cab is lit, it's not available, and even that's no guarantee you'll get one to stop. Skinny women were running out in the middle of Sixth Avenue jumping around trying to flag them down, but I was too slow and tired for such aerobics. Steve had to do it for me. And you know the drama associated with a black man trying to get a cab. They sped up when he stepped out there and put his hand in the air. Finally I got a second wind, stepped out, and did my thing. I was in the middle of the street, pissed because cabs were whizzing by, and when one did finally slow down long enough for us to hop in, I took a look and noticed that two BIG girls could never catch one cab together. We'd never fit. Shit, neither would a F.A.T. girl and a thin man. Which meant that Steve was going to have to sit up front, because there's no sliding in when you're THICK. You've got to roll in and hope there's room enough with that thick bullet-proof partition and your THICK self, and all your BIG shopping bags. Before I could get in good and slam the door, the cabbie was punching the meter, then took off like it was a robbery and he was driving the getaway car. By the time we got to the hotel, I was dizzy.

But working the Apollo is well worth the craziness of the city. I love New Yorkers—baby, they keep it realer than real. When we taped the first few shows, all my BIG sisters came out and represented, and I designated the first few rows just for them, because we don't get to be treated like Queens very often. I loved seeing that many BIG girls in one spot, cheering on another sister in size. In between takes, they were helping me with the TelePrompTer, making sure my clothes fit right, and shouting out the most wonderful words of support. And when the time came to Wop someone off that stage, BIG girls represented. Baby, there's something magical about the Apollo and about seeing so many of my people in one place, displaying so much talent. It's the gig of a lifetime, and so is experiencing it in the city that's so nice they had to name it twice. I know it's a cliché, but I too love New York.

I didn't love leaving and having to take Amtrak, though. It's only a mere four hours from the city to Baltimore, but it was my first—and last—time seeing the world from the vantage point of a train. At first I thought that a train ride would be a relaxing way to get home. This was when money was too tight to mention. Once again, I was in a hurry and starved. Now train fare is far worse than plane fare, but at least it's hot. Shit, a couple of BIG girls could take a dining car down. Thank God it was a short ride. When the conductor handed me the menu, potato chips were listed as an appetizer, a bologna sandwich was an entrée, and Oreo cookies were listed as dessert. I didn't want any of that shit, but potato chips can taste like steak if eaten at the right time, and this was one of those times. And it wouldn't have been so bad eating Ruffles if I hadn't been able to look out the window and see the golden arches of McDonald's in the distance, or people eating all sorts of gourmet meals, while all you can do is look and wave. And don't even get me started on the seats. On trains you sit facing each other, so crazy movements get noticed—by everyone. But if you think train and plane seats are bad, try bunking in one of those tight-ass cabins on a cruise ship. They're closets, and I ain't talkin' walk-in.

A year or so ago, I went on a four-day cruise to Mexico. Now, I used to watch *The Love Boat*, and everyone always seemed to be having such a good time. After frolicking on the deck all day, bartender Isaac Washington always seemed to end up with a honey in his cabin, or Captain Merrill Stubing's palatial quarters always seemed like the place to kick it. Well, we damn sure weren't on the Love Boat. It felt more like a tugboat. I said bon voyage to the family, opened the door to the cabin, and got the shock of my life. The shit was about the size of a box—a shoebox. I swear I had to enter sideways just to get in, and my date, who was six-four, had to bend down to get in—and this was a deluxe suite. He spent the entire time hunched over, and I was sideways. We found an interesting way to make that shit work, though. I guess small quarters are the way they force folks to mix and mingle, and it worked—I got seasick trying to kick it in that nook. Ordinarily, I like to get out and socialize, but salsa dancing just ain't a BIG person's cup of tea. Hell, no one can dip us. Let's do something easy like the Electric Slide, or the hustle. And why must we be assigned to eat with folks we don't know? We wanted to spend a nice quiet dinner together, but we were forced to dine with a group of folks who were about forty years older than we were. The only saving grace was the buffets.

And speaking of cruise food: I love that there's plenty of it and that it's available whenever I want it, but I can tell there isn't a soul sister in the kitchen. The shit is bland. I'm not complaining, though; with that much free grub, believe me, I can find creative ways to doctor it up. Listen, BIG eaters, bypass those shrimp at the omelet station and go for the prawns on ice, a few sprigs of broccoli at the salad station, a handful of bacon in a chafing dish, and any other choice ingredients that strike your fancy, and have the chef toss all of it together for an even tastier—and more filling—breakfast. But if a soulful breakfast on the high seas is what you're looking for, sign up for one of those black cruises. Baby, the folks who put those Festival at Sea and Tom Joyner cruises together know how to get their party on—and it's a party with a purpose. The purpose is to Electric Slide on the deck all day, play bid whiz all night, attend your Greek fraternities' step shows, and gorge on soul-food buffets at all hours of the day and night. What's the purpose of all that, you ask? To tire you out so that by the time you get to that little bunk of a room, you'll be so wiped out it won't matter how small it is. And you'll have to come home and rest from your activity-packed vacation.

But nothing beats the vacations you get at some of these new mega resorts, and Las Vegas is the king of them. When the Queens of Comedy performed in Sin City, we stayed at the MGM Grand, and it seemed like there was a restaurant every five steps. After each night's performance, the other ladies were hightailing it to the blackjack and craps tables, but not me. I was trying to find a table to get my eat on. That's why I don't mind getting lost at the Bellagio, Mandalay Bay, or the Venetian—no matter how lost you get, there's always a five-dollar buffet somewhere along the journey where one can take a snack break, and it's open at all hours of the day and night. At the Atlantis resort in the Bahamas, I thought I'd died and gone to heaven. The place is HUGE, but what I love most is not the GIGANTIC beach, not the lagoon, and not even that MASSIVE water slide. I like that they've taken into consideration that we need restaurants, and plenty of them. They don't make us walk a country mile just to find a coffee shop. Every few feet there's a snack bar, a hot-dog hut, or a drink stand where we can get something to quench our thirst. And if you're tired after lounging by the pool all day, they've also made it easy to just grab a drink and some appetizers at swim-up bars, or a strapping young hunk who's more than happy to serve you with a smile. Yeah, mon, it is better in the Bahamas, and in Jamaica, too. No wonder Stella went there to get her groove back. Baby, West Indians appreciate the THICKNESS of sisters, and it ain't hated, it's celebrated. But what I really celebrate when I'm there are the all-inclusive resorts where you pay one price and eat—and drink—as much as you want. For about a year, I woke up every morning at

3:00 A.M. Los Angeles time to go on the air as a morning DJ at WHUR in Washington, D.C. Part of the job was broadcasting from some fun, tropical locales. And when you come to a place like Jamaica, the locals love to treat you, drive you, and feed you. We'd be on the air, and they'd be bringing plates of food for us to enjoy. And it would be grilled steak and chicken, and lobsters right out of the Atlantic Ocean. You can't get any better service than that. Everything was no problem, mon.

Proper accommodations can definitely be a BIG problem. In fact, a small room—like the one on that cruise ship—will fuck up a perfectly good vacation, and so can a long-ass walk to a room. When we played Vegas, I noticed that Sommore, Miss Laura, and Adele Givens's rooms were near the elevator, and mine was waaaaaaaaaaaaaaay down the hall. Every night, when it was time to turn in, they got to their rooms in no time, but it seemed to take me ten minutes just to find the right tower. And after being onstage all night, and on the town partying until the wee hours of the morning, those damn towers start to all look alike. A couple of times, not only did I stumble into the wrong tower, hell, I stumbled into the wrong hotel. I thought they were trying to be smart and was about to raise hell until I learned that suites are usually at the end of the hall. The other ladies were walking just as far as I was, but at a more rapid pace.

Pace yourself if the Ritz-Carlton is your stop, though. Oh, it's a nice hotel, but you'll pay a ton for those tiny rooms, and for that much money, and after we've traveled all night, the least they could do is have an early check-in available. Sitting in a lobby half the morning after you've attempted to sleep on an airplane all night isn't cool. I tried to lay down on a Ritz-Carlton bed once and nearly got a concussion. That damn mattress was hard as a rock, and the towels are a problem, too.

The same problem as the airplane blankets—if you've got hips and ass, you can tug until it's tattered, but it still ain't gonna give. That's why I give specific instructions about what a hotel must have if I'm going to stay there. It must have twenty-four-hour room service. Because after you've gotten busy, if you know what I mean, you may want to get busy with a cheese-burger and fries and the words "Room service is closed" can be some upsetting news. A walk-in shower or a BIG bathtub is also a must-have, preferably one that's BIG enough for two in case a romantic rendezvous is on the agenda. Closet space is vital, too. I've stayed in some of these luxury hotels and couldn't even close the closet door because my clothes and shoes were too BIG to fit. And last but certainly not least, a Queen shouldn't sleep on anything less than a Queen-size bed. Fuck a double. Don't even try a twin. We need a com-fortable night's sleep and don't want half of our bodies to be crushed up against the wall trying not to fall out. But don't fret. If you happen to find yourself stuck in a hotel that doesn't offer the amenities you desire, do what Queen of Comedy Miss Laura taught me. Go to a restaurant, ask them to wrap your food in aluminum foil, take it back to the hotel, set up the ironing board, and plug in the iron. Turn it upside down and voilà, you've got an instant hot plate. See, you've got to be resourceful, ladies.

After living in hotels and flying on airplanes, every now and then I like to rejuvenate by spending a relaxing day at the spa. I've learned to take care of myself, and a massage always relieves the stress of my hectic life. Usually I go with girl-friends, but once, on a whim, I jumped into the car by myself and headed to a destination spa about an hour outside L.A. I had booked an entire day of pampering and was ready for my deep-tissue massage, classic deep cleansing facial, and deluxe manicure and pedicure. When I checked in, the staff was polite, but I could tell they weren't expecting me to be 220 pounds. After a thirty-minute wait, they showed me to the massage room, told me to put on the robe behind the door and lie down on the table, and my masseuse would be in shortly. Ready to get started, I got undressed and attempted to put on the robe. They must have gotten it from Gap Kids because I couldn't fit in the damn thing. I calmly requested an XXL. This sent the entire place into pandemonium. They acted like it was the first time a F.A.T. client had ever set foot in the place—like BIG girls don't like to get rubbed down, too. Now mind you, I'm supposed to be getting relaxed, but this runaround was making me tense. I was ready for my sixty-minute massage, but just as the masseuse was getting into it, the rubdown stopped abruptly. She was done—ten minutes early. I told her she owed me ten more minutes, but she informed me that the ten minutes it took for them to find me a proper size robe was deducted from my time. What the hell is that about? First of all, we've got more to rub, so our massages should be two hours; second, who's fault is it that my robe didn't fit? After that one treatment, I got dressed, left that place in a huff, and drove home with the worst case of road rage ever.

But nothing could compare to the rage I felt toward Steve when he booked me the stand-up gig from hell, or should I say, to hell. Before promoters flew me in for shows, Steve had me on the road driving from gig to gig. You've heard of musicians going out on twenty-city tours? Well, back in the day, Steve put together what was—and probably still is—the smallest tour in the history of tours, a three-city tour. Yep, you read right. It was Chicago, Atlanta, and Columbia, South Carolina. He was proud of himself, too. And we didn't stay on the road, driving from city to city. We worked Monday through Friday, then hit the road on Friday after work. We'd arrive in each city early Saturday morning, play the venue, then turn around and be back home early Sunday morning. Hey, say what you want, that was the best we could do at the time, and I was grateful for it, and for those early audiences who came out to see me in these little venues. But after these road tours, I grew to hate car trips—probably because of a particular one.

I was living in Atlanta and working for MCI by day, but at night and on the weekends I was onstage, performing. Now, y'all know me, performing is my life, but a F.A.T. black woman performing for the Ku Klux Klan? This had to be a first. It was late on a Friday evening, and Steve was in Baltimore. He had gotten a call from a booking agent inquiring about my availability for a gig the following week. Now, this was BIG. Steve put the man on hold (he had to make it seem like I was a BIG act and had lots of offers), then came back to the phone and told him I was available. The agent asked for a head shot, but Steve lied and told the man we'd run out. The truth was, we didn't have any. But that didn't seem to bother the agent. So he booked me sight unseen on a gig down in Birmingham, Alabama, just two hours outside Atlanta. When Steve called to fill me in on the details, I told him no problem, I'll just jump into the car, do the gig, and drive back that night. Now, the backwoods of Alabama are no joke. So imagine my horror when I followed the directions, and they led to a dirt road cutoff. I thought to myself, what the hell has Steve gotten me into now?

When I finally found the place, I swear it was a scene straight out of *Mississippi Burning*. It was a barn. Hay. And when I opened the door, a bunch of country bumpkins in cowboy boots and plaid shirts, chugging beer. The sounds of "hee haw" flowed freely. They might as well have thrown a couple of banjos into the mix and a Confederate flag—I swear, the minute I walked in, I thought I heard one of them say, "Lookahere at what the cat done dragged in." It looked like a Klan meeting in progress. This gig was turning into a joke within itself. Oh, and remember that Confederate flag I was talking about? It was proudly on display—over the stage. For more than a moment, I thought about hightailing it out of there, but Steve had arranged for them to pay me in cash, and I didn't have enough gas or money to get back home. They say, never let 'em see you sweat, but I can't lie. I was scared to death. I had to think quickly and make the best of a bad situation. These hillbillies were paying customers, and I was there to give them a show. Plus, I thought about the consequences of not being funny, so I said a quick prayer and opened with, "Y'all will not hang my F.A.T. black ass in here tonight, I'm about to do some mother-fuckin' jokes." And for an hour I told every one I knew, and even made up a few.

When the first toothless joker slapped his knee, I knew it was gonna be all right. That was one of the toughest nights—and crowds—of my life, but those rednecks laughed heartily—and paid on time. The money wasn't in my hot hands two seconds before I hightailed it out of there. And, on the drive back, two valuable lessons came to mind: (1) Never judge a redneck by his red neck. You damn sure wouldn't catch me with this crowd after sundown, but for an hour and a half these were paying customers who deserved a good show regardless of their racist attitudes. (2) Trying to get this crowd to laugh was the bottom line, and when they did, I knew then that my knack for making people—all people—laugh was a gift from God. I got the hell out of there, stopped at a well-lit gas station on the main highway, called Steve in Baltimore, and fired his ass.

But he was back on the payroll in no time when he negotiated one of the most amazing—and eye-opening—experiences of my life. In 1997 Steve received a call from a television show in Johannesburg, South Africa, called *It's a Funny Country*, the South African equivalent of *Showtime at the Apollo*. They wanted me to come over and do stand-up, so we embarked on a ten-day journey where I made history as the first black woman to ever perform on the show. Nothing beats the feeling of going to Africa. It's something everyone should do at some point in life. The moment we got off the airplane, everyone greeted us with open arms. And the women, BABY, the women were ROBUST, just like me. And they hugged me and said, "Welcome, my sister." It felt good to be home in the Motherland, but what made the trip even more memorable wasn't the fact that I was the first black woman to do my comedy on South Africa's most popular show, not the standing ovation, not the fact that I had finally made it here—it was because for the first time, I wasn't a BIG girl trying to fit into a small world. I was in the land of the original BIG, BEAUTI-FUL WOMEN—and I was one of them! That's right—over there, unless you're carrying 200 pounds or more, they aren't checkin' for you, and I LOVE THAT!

After the performance Steve and I were invited to go on a safari. Now, we're two folks from Baltimore, Maryland, but being the adventurers that we are, we said, "Cool." We didn't know what the hell to expect, so when they picked us up, we were dressed like we were going out for a day at the races. I had on a sundress and heels, and Steve broke out with a pair of 120 wool pants and a linen shirt. We thought we were doin' it. Nobody told us that we'd be riding through the jungle with armed escorts who were prepared to shoot if the animals got a little too close to the car. The entire experience was amazing—and hot as hell—but I will never forget a monkey we passed, chillin' on a rock. The minute he spotted Steve and me, I swear it seemed like he looked us up and down, shook his head, then scratched his behind, like, Where do those two fools think they're going? We're in the middle of the jungle, and one of them has on a pair of wool pants. Steve and I laugh about that to this day. Whatever the adventure, it's always a learning experience.

But some experiences are just meant to be fun. When time permits, I love to take vacations with my son. Because I'm a BIG kid at heart, we always end up at Six Flags Magic Mountain, or some other theme or water park. But amusement parks aren't designed for 200-pound kids. Roller coasters have gotten to be scary. Faster. Higher. Longer. But damn it, the seats are smaller. After they push the bar down over your stomach, you don't have time to be scared because you're too busy trying to breathe. That's why water parks are fun. You don't have to worry about getting a seat; all you have to do is find a spot and know how to float.

But whether you choose to float on the water, see the world from the skies, or on a long car ride, just do it. Sure, it's a crazy, crazy world, but I'm truly blessed to have gotten a chance to experience it from every vantage point there is. And though the travel industry has a lot of catching up to do when it comes to accommodating us, I still say plan a trip, take a cruise, get out there and see the world. Slowly but surely, just like with the fashion industry, the travel industry will begin to realize that America is a FATTER place, and what a beautiful place it is.

Mo'Nique's Guide to Getting the Best Grub in Airports

Traveling can be tough, especially if you're F.A.T. But, if you gotta go, at least know where to get the best grub:

ATLANTA, HARTSFIELD INTERNATIONAL

ATRIUM: Wendy's, Houlihan's

CONCOURSE A: Cinnabon, Ben & Jerry's Ice Cream, Domino's Pizza

CONCOURSE B: Popeye's Chicken, Sbarro

BOSTON, LOGAN AIRPORT

TERMINAL B: Legal Sea Foods Café, Auntie Anne's Pretzels, Dunkin' Donuts, Sbarro, TCBY

TERMINAL C: Legal Sea Foods Restaurant, Dunkin' Donuts, TCBY

TERMINAL D: Dunkin' Donuts

TERMINAL E: Sbarro

CHICAGO, O'HARE INTERNATIONAL

TERMINAL 1: Wolfgang Pucks, Panda Express

DETROIT/WAYNE COUNTY AIRPORT

GATE A74: Edy's Ice Cream

GATE B5: Orville & Wilbur's Wings

GATE A74: Taco Bell

CENTRAL LINK AREA: Little Caesar's Pizza, TCBY

GATE A21: Gayle's Chocolates

GATE B5: Pasta Pasta

GATE A60: A&W

DALLAS/FORT WORTH INTERNATIONAL

TERMINAL A: Taco Bell (Gate A13), Chick Fil-A (Gate A25), TGI Friday's (Gate A22), Auntie Anne's Pretzels (Gates A25, A39)

TERMINAL B: Auntie Anne's Pretzels (Gate B5), Chili's Too (Gate B19), I Can't Believe It's Yogurt (Gate B29), Sbarro (Gate B4)

TERMINAL C: Wendy's (Gate C14), Häagen-Dazs (Gate C17), I Can't Believe It's Yogurt (Gate C24), Taco Bell (Gate C14), Pizza Hut (Gates C6, 20)

TERMINAL E: Auntie Anne's Pretzels (Gate E16), Dickey's BBQ (Gate E12), Häagen-Dazs (E15, E27), TGI Fridays (E17), Taco Bell (Gates E5,15)

HOUSTON INTERCONTINENTAL AIRPORT

CONCOURSE B: Chili's

CONCOURSE C: Popeye's, Subway, Pretzelmania, Taco Bell, Wendy's

NEW ORLEANS AIRPORT

TERMINAL A: Ben & Jerry's Ice Cream

TERMINAL C: Häagen-Dazs

TERMINAL D: Häagen-Dazs

NEW YORK, JOHN F. KENNEDY AIRPORT

TERMINAL 3: Sbarro, Chili's

TERMINAL 4: Krispy Kreme

TERMINAL 8: Sbarro

TERMINAL 9: Sbarro, TGI Friday's

NEW YORK, LAGUARDIA AIRPORT

CENTRAL TERMINAL: Sbarro, Wendy's, Pretzel Time

DELTA TERMINAL: Sbarro Express

USAIRWAYS TERMINAL: Everything Yogurt, Sbarro, David's Cookies

SEATTLE/TACOMA AIRPORT

MAIN TERMINAL NORTH SATELLITE: Cinnabon, Dreyer's Ice Cream/See's Candy

CONCOURSE B: Pizza Hut

CONCOURSE C: Pretzelmania, Taco Bell, TCBY Treats

CONCOURSE D: Pretzelmania

WASHINGTON, D.C., RONALD REAGAN NATIONAL AIRPORT

TERMINAL A: Jerry's Subs & Pizza

TERMINAL C: Auntie Anne's Pretzels, TGI Friday's, Cheesecake Factory, California Pizza Kitchen

Mo'Nique's Favorite Web Sites

www.1monique.com	The official Mo'Nique Web site for the latest in tours and information.
www.upn.com	For information on *The Parkers* and other UPN shows.
www.tolerance.org	A Web site designed to fight hate and promote tolerance.
www.naafa.org	National Association to Advance FAT Acceptance.
www.obesitylaw.com	Obesity Law and Advocacy Center.
www.cswd.org	Council on Size and Weight Discrimination.
www.clubcurves.com	Where full-figured sisters go to mix it up with those who appreciate curves.
www.fredericks.com	Frederick's of Hollywood, for sexy lingerie and clothing in plus sizes.
www.blackvoices.com	Your ticket to what's hot on the Web.

www.largefeet.com	Friedman's Shoes located in Atlanta is the on-the-Web-spot for women's shoes in sizes seven to thirteen.
www.lanebryant.com	The most recognized name in plus-size fashions.
www.gracestyle.com	The on-line magazine for full-figured women.